THE PSYCHOPATH'S BIBLE
FOR THE EXTREME INDIVIDUAL

THE PSYCHOPATH'S BIBLE

FOR THE EXTREME INDIVIDUAL

by
Christopher S. Hyatt, Ph.D.

With Dr. Jack Willis
Foreword by Nicholas Tharcher

NEW FALCON PUBLICATIONS
TEMPE, ARIZONA, U.S.A.

International Standard Book Number: 1-56184-174-9
Library of Congress Catalog Card Number: 94-69287

First pre-publication edition of 100 copies
(originally titled *The Toxick Magician*)
printed by Dagon Productions
distributed by Robert F. Williams, Jr. 1994 C.E.

Second Revised Edition 2000 C.E.

Third Expanded & Revised Edition 2003 C.E.
Fourth Printing 2004 C.E.
Fifth Printing 2006 C.E.

Cover Art by Linda Joyce Franks
Interior artwork by S. Jason Black
plus one by Zehm Alohim (who is he, anyway?);
"The Devil & Dr. Hyatt" by Jonathan Sellers

The paper used in this publication meets the minimum requirements of the American National Standard for Permanence of Paper for Printed Library Materials Z39.48-1984

Address all inquiries to:
NEW FALCON PUBLICATIONS
1739 East Broadway Road #1-277
Tempe, AZ 85282 U.S.A.
(or)
320 East Charleston Blvd. #286-204
Las Vegas, NV 89104 U.S.A.
website: http://www.newfalcon.com
email: info@newfalcon.com

Dedicated to
Robert F. Williams, Jr.

One of the Best Men We Had

And coll it "THE PSYCHOPATH'S BIBLE"

THE DEVIL AND DR. HYATT.

Disclaimer

Everything in this book is for amusement purposes only. It is all a lie. If you are foolish enough to employ the concepts or exercises, you do so at your own risk. Neither the authors nor the publisher recommend anything. Check with your lawyer, doctor and local police before following any of the suggestions herein.

Acknowledgements

Dr. Hyatt would like to express his thanks to Zehm Alohim, Kelli Holloran, S. Jason Black, Jon Sellers of Antiquities of the Illuminati, Doug Grant and so many more who provided grist for his mill; however, he won't because he is a selfish, self-centered son of a bitch...
— The Publisher

P.S. Every mistake, intentional or otherwise, is the fault of the reader.
— Dr. Hyatt

The Essence of This Book

A. Accept that you are less than you can be and that you want to be more.

B. Remove all ideas—positive or negative—about yourself.

C. If you have the will, then do everything which makes you stronger and stop everything that makes you weaker.

D. The means to accomplish this is contained within......

Primary to our understanding of the Extreme Individual is the will to overcome anything which prevents us from reaching our own personal ideal. In opposition to the *will to overcome* is the fear of losing what we have.

When we feel safe, our tendency is to reach out to create—to fulfill our wildest dreams—to challenge the world. Extreme Individuals, however, don't wait to feel safe; they simply proceed to overcome obstacles which stand in their way of self expansion, of going beyond what they are and what they feel. Man wants to triumph, to be victorious in his life and some men want and need this more than others. These are the Extreme Individuals, those who push the boundaries of the ordinary.

Table of Contents

Manual I:
The Toxick Magician
37

Manual II: Toxick Calculus:
The Process of De-Education
101

Manual III:
The No-Where University, Sometimes Called P.U.
169

Appendices
195

foreword

Psychopath: A person with an antisocial personality disorder, especially one manifested in aggressive, perverted, criminal, or amoral behavior.
— *The American Heritage Dictionary*

It's good to be the king.
— Mel Brooks

For years the market has been flooded with books filled with "sweetness and light." This is not one of them.

Most people will characterize this book as evil, malevolent, unprincipled, wicked and pessimistic. It is all of that—and worse.

It is an "evil" book with "evil" ideas. This is necessarily so because this book tells the truth. Truth is always characterized as "evil."

In some ways this is a book of social philosophy; in other ways it is a book of technique. Which it is for you may depend more on your attitude than on anything else.

The average person will not even finish the Introduction. After a page or two, most will put it down and return to the mush of the TV set. We recommend that you do so. *This book is toxic!*[1]

Most people will be appalled by this book. Many will ignore or dismiss its message as too horrifying even to acknowledge. This is exactly what we want: it advances the Work. (Indeed, if you are one of the rare few who do not see it thus, we congratulate you as

---

[1] The weak-minded reader might see this as a dare and read on anyway. Good. That's what we want. On the other hand, you might see right through this transparent challenge, resent being told what to do—as you should—and stop now before you waste your precious time and money. Good. That's what we want. (If you *do* read on, the words "double bind" might come to mind from time to time.) By the way, we've included lots of footnotes in this Foreword to provide an illusion of academic pseudo-intellectualism.

you are probably already a Master and you are *already* advancing the Work.)

We can state with confidence that most people will be appalled (or worse) because we have already seen it happen. We have noticed that quite a few of the brave souls who read through the earlier editions (the first of which was titled *The Toxick Magician*), and those who helped "test drive" this greatly expanded version, have remarked that the first chapters seemed rather easy to take—despite our dire warnings. Indeed, it seemed to them that these first chapters seemed rather light-hearted, even amusing. And then, sometimes quite suddenly, they would remark that they felt something change within themselves, that it seemed that the tone of the book itself changed and that they began to feel disturbed—sometimes *very* disturbed. Whether it was the reader or the book itself that changed we leave for you to decide.

You might even do this experiment for yourself: read the first five chapters or so. See if they seem "easy to take." Then keep reading and see if you feel a difference, perhaps a greater sense of dread and malevolence. If you do, go back and reread those first chapters again. Do they still seem as easy to take?

Many writers claim to be concerned with the lamentable condition of the human species and purport to present the means to bring man to a "higher state" of consciousness or evolution, or some such. Dr. Hyatt claims nothing of the sort. Rather, this book is intended as an instruction book for the psychopath,[2] the sort of person who cares nothing for the "advancement" of the species.

---

[2] For those who wonder about the difference between the terms "psychopath" and "sociopath," please note that both the dictionary and psychiatric definitions of the two words are now literally identical. (Indeed, they are now referred to as "Antisocial Personality Disorder.") This was

Much has been written *about* the psychopath but very little has been written *for* the psychopath.[3] Perhaps the best-known are Sun Wu's *Sun Tzu the Art of War* and Niccolò Machiavelli's *The Prince* (1532), both written for the political psychopath. (At one time we considered titling this book *The New Prince: Machiavelli Revisited* in homage to Machiavelli's work even though we personally despise all those in and around the political field.)

Though (probably) not written specifically for the psychopath, Eric Hoffer's *The True Believer: Thoughts on the Nature of Mass Movements* (1951) is essential reading for the practitioner.

We are aware of few other useful titles in the non-fiction arena—not in psychology or even in political "science"—except for a few books classified in the "salesmanship" category. Some of Robert J. Ringer's work, such as *Winning Through Intimidation* and *Looking Out For No. 1* (both reissued in 1993) are particularly useful. (As Mr. Ringer so clearly points out, these are not salesmanship books at all. Nonetheless, hardly anyone seems to believe him. To us, this is an indication that Mr. Ringer is a great Master. One of the axioms of life is this: even if you tell the truth—perhaps *because* you tell the truth—no one will believe you.)

Most commonly the psychopath has been depicted in a positive way only in fiction—the popularity of which emphasizes the moth-to-the-flame fascination most people have for the breed.

---

not always so. We speculate that the merging of these two terms has been done for the convenience of those in the psychiatric and criminal justice systems so that they need only consider behavior and not internal psychological factors.

[3] Though useful for all psychopaths, this book is particularly written for the group of psychopaths we consider the best and highest of all—in our terms. We call them "Toxick Magicians." More about that later.

(Though we focus mainly on movies, if you like to read you might want to keep in mind that many of the movies we mention—here and in Appendix I—were derived from books—some good, some bad. Further some useful books have not been made into movies at all; Ayn Rand's *Atlas Shrugged* (1957), is an excellent example.)

You can find a few comedies (mostly among older British films); these include *The Magic Christian* (1969), *School for Scoundrels* (1960) and *The Captain's Paradise* (1954). You can also find a few comedy/dramas (notably *The Sting* (1973), and *Butch Cassidy and the Sundance Kid* (1969)—which are unquestionably among the best-loved psychopath movies ever made). However, most works which depict psychopaths are straight dramas. Among these are such excellent movies as *Point Break* (in our view, one of the purest and best of its kind) and the ever-popular *Silence of the Lambs*.[4]

We believe that the most significant quality which makes many of these works so appealing is that the hero–psychopath is, at least to a large extent, *conscious* of his values and *deliberate* in his actions.[5] (Contrast the unconsciously driven nut-cases in suspense/terror/horror movies like *The Hand That Rocks the Cradle* (1992), and its numerous clones; these characters seem to inspire little or no sympathy with the audience.)

---

[4] *Silence of the Lambs* is an example of an excellent movie derived from an excellent book (i.e., the book of the same name by Thomas Harris). The story of Hannibal Lecter's earlier "activities," *Red Dragon* (1981) was also quite good. Two decent movies were derived from the book: *Manhunter* (1986), and *Red Dragon* (2002). The third book in the Lecter series, *Hannibal*, was published in 1999 and made into a movie in 2000; both the book and the movie were less well-received than the others. Nonetheless, it seems clear that after many years, Lecter, his liver, fava beans, and Chianti are still treasured.

[5] The *conscious* psychopath is often seen as very "real" and frequently as a rather sympathetic character. This is certainly true for the fictional psychopath, and is also true for the real-life psychopath much more often than most people would like to admit.

Throughout history—throughout most of the world—real, live psychopaths have gotten a bad rap. That is quite understandable since almost all of the world's religious and social philosophies have little use for the individual except as a tool to be placed in service to their notion of something else: "God," or the "collective," or the "higher good," or some other equally undefinable term. Only rarely, such as in Zen, some aspects of Tibetan Buddhism and Hinduism, and some schools of Existentialism, is the truly autonomous individual considered primal.

To most of the world, anyone who holds himself apart from the herd (*especially* in the psychological sense) is, *at least*, highly suspect and probably blasphemous, heretical and criminal. (Almost every definition of the term psychopath includes the word "criminal" as one of its key characteristics.)

Who are held up to the world as archetypal examples of psychopaths? Almost without exception they are of the *violent* criminal variety: "crazed loners," "terrorists," "spree killers," "mass murderers" and "serial killers" are popular characterizations today.[6] ("Satanists," "witches" and their ilk get a play from time to time but haven't really caught on.[7])

---

[6] Note that all of these categories are highly stylized and serve to dehumanize the individuals about which they speak. This is a common—and important—methodology when referring to "enemies."

[7] One can make a strong case that modern psychiatry is simply a pseudo-scientific replacement for, and extension of, the witchhunts and inquisitions of earlier times. The brilliant psychiatrist (yes, psychiatrist!) Thomas Szasz has done just that. See *The Manufacture of Madness: A Comparative Study of the Inquisition and the Mental Health Movement* (Harper and Row, 1970).

People in the political and propaganda (i.e., news) businesses love examples of this kind: it gives them a golden opportunity to rabble-rouse and pontificate.

Frequently they will describe the actions of these "terrible people" as "incomprehensible." When motivations are considered at all, such people are usually seen as demented, clinically insane, sexually frustrated, politically fanatical, or simply as incompetent malcontents. Then comes the litany of assertions of "explanations" for their behavior—books, music, video games, television, movies, the Internet (or any relatively new technology), pornography, satanism, "society," etc., etc. *ad nauseam*.

Historically, certain conquerors and political figures (e.g., Hitler, Napoleon, Stalin) and competitors to "legitimate governments" (e.g., organized crime figures such as Jesse James, Al Capone, John Dillinger and John Gotti[8]) have been characterized as psychopaths.

This focus on the violent psychopath may be dramatic, but it is also rather narrow. In a sense, to isolate one's focus to figures such as these is like saying that "Christians" are typified by Torquemada and Jim Jones. (Come to think of it, there are millions—perhaps billions—of people on this planet who would agree with such a characterization of Christianity. Including us.)

In reality, there are many operating psychopaths who never reach the public eye. Some are never identified as such because they are successful at what they do (i.e., they don't get caught). Many more are never characterized as psychopaths because they do not exercise *unacceptable* criminal behavior (remember that criminal behavior—especially *violent* criminal behavior—is usually considered one of the essential, defining characteristics of the psychopath) and are thus considered acceptable, even valuable, members of society. Many businessmen, lawyers, doctors, and politicians fall into this group. (It has often been said that Al

---

[8] It seems interesting to us that many of these "criminals" were viewed as heroic figures by many of the people of their time.

Capone would have been a great success in the "legitimate" business world if he had not become involved in "criminal" activities. This should come as no great surprise considering that many of the businesses in which Capone and others of his time were engaged—for example, the sale of alcohol and other chemicals, gambling, moneylending and prostitution—were then, and are today, defined as "legitimate" or "criminal" only by the circumstances of geography.)

Considering the amount of focus that is expended on the violent psychopath, it appears interesting to us that there really seem to be very few operating psychopaths in these traditionally accepted "nut- group" categories. For example, according to the FBI, there are probably no more than thirty-five "serial killers" operating in the U.S. at any given time.[9]

Also, according to the FBI, virtually all assertions of the existence of any organized, violent "Satanic" conspiracies have proven to be unfounded.

Even more significant to us, however, is the rare occurrence of relatively large-scale violent acts[10] initiated by individuals or small groups: "terrorist" acts like the two attacks on the World Trade Center in New York, the bombng of the Federal Building in Oklahoma City, "mass murders," airplane bombings, etc. seem to us rather rare (and, incidentally, often rather incompetently executed).[11] Indeed, with all the hype about the alleged power, determination, organization and resources of certain "terrorist groups,"

---

[9] Some academic sources claim as many as two hundred and some claim that the number is rising. In any case, however, the whole thing seems like small potatoes.

[10] This statement, of course, deliberately excludes the perpetrators of *really* large-scale violent acts: i.e., governments.

[11] Each such occurrence, of course, receives an enormous amount of publicity and hand-wringing. But let's be honest: add it all up and there really have been very few incidents of this kind, worldwide, throughout all of human history. Moreover, the total number of people injured and killed in all these incidents put together amounts to less than a pimple on the ass of any minor-league governmentally-inspired war.

it seems particularly strange to us that, as of this writing, no one has yet done something *really* dramatic such as setting off a nuclear bomb in Washington, D.C. Are all these "psychopaths" really so incompetent?[12]

It is worth noting that some people have suggested that, because we have written about the violent psychopath, we are somehow encouraging such behavior. *Nothing could be further from the truth!!* We wish to make it absolutely clear that we do not condone the initiation of violence to achieve any end, by anyone, at any time, in any place, in any way. For us, there is one fundamental rule of interpersonal behavior: *it is absolutely unacceptable to initiate violence under any circumstances.* (In case you wonder if we have joined the sweetness-and-light, turn-the-other-cheek crowd, consider the significance of the word "initiate.")

Clinical Definitions

Now that that's out of the way, what does the *academic* world say about the psychopath? Here are some "accepted" definitions.

From the *American Heritage Dictionary*: Psychopath: "A person with an *antisocial personality disorder,* especially one manifested in aggressive, perverted, criminal, or amoral behavior." [Emphasis added]

---

[12] Some people feel that the rarity of such deeds suggests (or even proves!) the existence of some sort of worldwide political/social conspiracy. Conspiracy theories appear to appeal to and console the human ego which longs for meaning and purpose and hates to accept that most people really *are* incompetent.

"Antisocial personality disorder" is a technical term in psychiatry which we will soon consider.

Note that all of the other adjectives are normative: "aggressive" (as compared to passive and compliant?), and "perverted, criminal, or amoral" which are all defined by what is "socially accepted."[13]

For a popularized definition of the psychopath we turn to Dr. Robert Hare, author of *Without Conscience: The Disturbing World of the Psychopaths Among Us*, who uses the following criteria to define a psychopath:

Glib and Superficial

"Psychopaths are often witty and articulate. They can be amusing and entertaining conversationalists, ready with a quick and clever comeback, and tell unlikely but convincing stories that cast themselves well and are often very likeable and charming."

Egocentric and Grandiose

"Psychopaths have a narcissistic and grossly inflated view of their self-worth and importance, a truly astonishing egocentricity and sense of entitlement, and see themselves as the center of the universe, as superior beings who are justified in living according to their own rules."

Lack of Remorse or Guilt

"Psychopaths show a stunning lack of concern for the devastating effects their actions have on others. Often they are completely forthright about the matter, calmly stating that they have no sense of guilt, are not sorry for the pain they have caused, and that there is no reason them for them to be concerned."

---

[13] "Socially accepted," of course, is not an "absolute"; it always refers to the mores at *a particular time and place*. No doubt you would laugh (and run) if a medical doctor said, "According to the customs of this society, you have an infection in your finger." But in psychiatry, this sort of diagnostic methodology is common and accepted.

Lack of Empathy

"One rapist, high on the 'Psychopathy Checklist', commented that he found it hard to empathize with his victims. Psychopaths view people as little more than objects to be used for their own gratification."

Deceitful and Manipulative

"With their powers of imagination in gear and focused on themselves, psychopaths appear amazingly unfazed by the possibility—or even by the certainty—of being found out. When caught in a lie or challenged with the truth, they are seldom perplexed or embarrassed—they simply change their stories or rework the facts so they appear to be consistent with the lie."

Shallow Emotions

"While at times they appear cold and unemotional, they are prone to dramatic, shallow and short-lived displays of feeling... Many clinicians have commented that the emotions of psychopaths are so shallow as to be little more than proto-emotions: primitive responses to immediate needs."

For a more detailed, clinical definition we can refer to the "bible" of psychiatry in the U.S., *The Diagnostic and Statistical Manual of Mental Disorders,* (DSM-IV™) 4th Edition, American Psychiatric Association, 1994.[14] So, what does DSM-IV™ say about "antisocial personality disorder"? (The extract below is only a

---

[14] If you've never picked up DSM-IV™, we strongly recommend that you do so. You'll find yourself in it. You'll find your friends and associates in it. You'll find your family members in it. Indeed, *you'll find everyone in it.* In other words, from the point of view of psychiatry, *everyone* has a "mental disorder." *For psychiatry, there is no such thing as mental health, only types and degrees of pathology!*

small part of a considerably longer [and really boring] "definition." We thought about including the whole thing for the sake of "academic correctness" but figured you'd fall asleep before getting to the good parts in the rest of this book. As far as we are concerned, what we have included is boring enough already and sufficient to make the point. All emphasis below has been added.)

The essential feature of Antisocial Personality Disorder is a pervasive pattern of disregard for, and violation of, the rights[15] of others that begins in childhood or early adolescence and continues into adulthood.

This pattern has also been referred to as psychopathy, sociopathy, or dyssocial personality disorder. ...Deceit and manipulation are central features...

...the individual must be at least age 18 years and must have had a history of some symptoms of Conduct Disorder before age 15 years.[16] Conduct Disorder involves a repetitive and persistent pattern of behavior in which the basic rights of others or major age-appropriate societal norms or rules are violated. The specific behaviors characteristic of Conduct Disorder fall into one of four categories: aggression to people and animals, destruction of property, deceitfulness or theft, or serious violation of rules.

The pattern of antisocial behavior continues into adulthood. [They] *fail to conform to social norms with respect to lawful behavior.* ...may repeatedly perform acts that are grounds for arrest...such as destroying property, harassing others, stealing, or pursuing illegal occupations. [They] *disregard the wishes, rights, or feelings of others.*[17] ...frequently deceitful and manipulative...to gain personal profit or pleasure... They

---

[15] Central as this is to the definition of psychopath, we are not aware of any definition of "rights" in DSM-IV™. Nonetheless, the common understanding of the term should suffice.

[16] So not to worry. There are no young psychopaths. Only psychopaths in training.

[17] Are we the only ones who find it weird that DSM-IV™ uses the words "wishes" and "feelings" in this sentence along with "rights." Disregarding the wishes or feelings of others is *pathology!?*

may repeatedly lie, use an alias, con others, or malinger.[18] A pattern of impulsivity... [They] tend to be irritable and aggressive and may repeatedly get into physical fights or commit acts of physical assault... ...also display a reckless disregard for the safety of themselves or others.

...tend to be *consistently and extremely irresponsible.* ...[They] show little remorse for the consequences of their acts. They may be indifferent to...having hurt, mistreated, or stolen from someone. ...[They] may blame the victims [sic] for being foolish, helpless, or deserving their fate; they may minimize the harmful consequences of their actions; or they may simply indicate complete indifference. They generally fail to compensate or make amends for their behavior. They may believe that everyone is out to "help number one" and that one should stop at nothing to avoid being pushed around.

Diagnostic Criteria

A. There is a pervasive pattern of disregard for and violation of the rights[19] of others occurring since age 15 years, as indicated by three (or more) of the following:

1. *failure to conform to social norms with respect to lawful behaviors* as indicated by repeatedly performing acts that are grounds for arrest

2. deceitfulness, as indicated by repeated lying, use of aliases, or conning others for personal profit or pleasure

3. impulsivity or failure to plan ahead

4. irritability and aggressiveness, as indicated by repeated physical fights or assaults

5. reckless disregard for safety of self or others

6. consistent irresponsibility, as indicated by repeated failure to sustain consistent work behavior or honor financial obligations

7. lack of remorse, as indicated by being indifferent to or rationalizing having hurt, mistreated, or stolen from another

B. The individual is at least age 18 years.

---

[18] Some might say that these are essential skills if one is to prosper—or even survive—in an insane world.

[19] This time it's only "rights," not "wishes" or "feelings."

C. There is evidence of Conduct Disorder with onset before age 15 years.

D. The occurrence of antisocial behavior is not exclusively during the course of Schizophrenia or a Manic Episode.

DSM-IV™ goes on with a list of "Associated Features and Disorders" including: "inflated and arrogant self-appraisal," "excessively opinionated, self-assured, or cocky."[20] Also the psychopath "may receive dishonorable discharges from the armed services, may fail to be self-supporting, may become impoverished or even homeless, or may spend many years in penal institutions" and are "more likely than people in the general population to die prematurely by violent means." (These are, indeed, some of the downsides if the psychopath doesn't do it well.)

Personally, I find the lesser-known definition of the World Health Organization (often used outside the U.S.) more interesting, snappy and concise:

From the ICD-10 Classification of Mental and Behavioural Disorders, World Health Organization, Geneva, 1992; F60.2 Dissocial (Antisocial) Personality Disorder [again, all emphasis added]:

Personality disorder, usually coming to attention because of a *gross disparity between behavior and the prevailing social norms,* and characterized by at least 3 of the following:

(a) callous unconcern for the feelings of others;

(b) gross and persistent attitude of irresponsibility and disregard for social norms, rules and obligations;

(c) incapacity to maintain enduring relationships, though having no difficulty in establishing them;

---

[20] In other words, while it's "good" to have "high self-esteem," don't exhibit more than a shrink considers acceptable.

(d) very low tolerance to frustration and a low threshold for discharge of aggression, including violence;

(e) incapacity to experience guilt and to profit from experience, particularly punishment;

(f) marked proneness to blame others, or to offer plausible rationalizations, for the behavior that has brought the patient into conflict with society.

There may also be persistent irritability as an associated feature. Conduct disorder during childhood and adolescence, though not invariably present, may further support the diagnosis.[21]

Why This Book?

With all these definitions and remarks behind us, it's time to get back to why this book was written. *This book was written to applaud, encourage and counsel the best among this wretched, sheeplike species called "man".* It pulls no punches, it makes no apologies, it minces no words. It applauds the rare individual who writes his own song, plays his own tune, and lives his own life.

In particular, it speaks to a particular breed of psychopath which we call interchangeably the "Toxick[22] Magician," the "Practitioner," or the "Manipulator". The most effective of these we refer to simply and reverentially as the "Master".

As with all psychopaths, he (or she[23]) recognizes the pathetic nature of the human condition and takes from it what he can. But

---

[21] For what it is worth, DSM-IV™ seems to consider Conduct Disorder more significant to the definition.

[22] The (mis)spelling is deliberate to emphasize the mindful nature and quality of the practitioner.

[23] For simplicity and convenience we use the pronoun "he" throughout this book to refer to all Toxick Magicians regardless of gender. We men-

the Toxick Magician goes further: he encourages *homo normalis* to live life according to his nature—the life Thomas Hobbes characterized as "brutish, nasty and short." [*Leviathan*, 1651] He encourages the human race to the precipice. He does what he can to help the species destroy itself and let nature get on with something(s) different.

He is a "magician" because he works his own will to achieve his own ends; he is "toxick" because destruction is his goal.[24] He is not afraid to be *deliberately* malicious and malevolent. From society's standpoint, he is the *worst* of the psychopaths because he does his Work *intentionally*. As such, he stands apart from their definitions—definitions which would like to emphasize the inability of the psychopath to control himself. The Toxick Magician is *conscious* of his actions and of his feelings. This makes him especially dangerous.

Most Toxick Magicians are made, not born. So why would anyone want to become one? There are many disadvantages. To name just a few: He requires immense concentration and years of ruthless work. He will probably not see the long-term results of his work. It can be a lonely life.

Still, it has its rewards. More than anything else, the Manipulator is *free*. He is free from the hallucinations that *homo normalis* insists we adopt and which men have so treasured all their lives: his eyes see only what is. He is free from the myths of safety and security: he knows that death awaits him. He is free from the delusion of the supremacy of the species: at his best, man is still pathetic and weak. He is free from the illusions of language, espe-

---

tion this because we certainly don't want to offend anyone or be accused of sexism.

[24] If you've ever seen a martial arts movie which features a master who is adept at something like a "Secret Death Touch" you have a useful working metaphor for the Toxick Magician. Like the martial arts Master, the Master Toxick Magician "touches" his victim and leaves. The victim never even knows he has been wounded, much less fatally so. Metaphorically speaking, of course.

cially "cause and effect" and "randomness": he can use words as tools when and where he chooses. He is free from the mirage of relationships: he knows where he is on the food chain. He is free from the pragmatic burdens the world insists on placing in the way of enjoyment: he laughs at the sheep and those in power alike and plots their downfall.

We do not expect to hear from many true, mature, operating, successful Masters since anonymity is essential to the success of their action. Nonetheless, some sole practitioners may want to come in for a "checkup"; some, perhaps, for companionship, or a break from the tedium of dealing with common man. Of course, we also want to hear from those who wish to become Practitioners—but take care: it will cost you a lot, perhaps much more than you are willing or prepared to pay. We know that very few will "make it." As the wise man said to those who sought enlightenment at his feet: "No more than 5% of you will gain anything; the rest of you are 'food.'" If you dare to spit at the odds, come ahead, but we advise against it. We suggest that you get rid of this book *now* before you are poisoned further. You have been warned.

If you are going to go ahead despite our warnings, we have a suggestion for both the aspiring and practicing Toxick Magician: buy two copies of this book. One, of course, is for your personal use. You should put the other away for your offspring or for future generations since, like Hoffer's *The True Believer*, this volume will likely go out of print all too soon; it would not surprise us if this book were *forced* out since it is so "dangerous."[25]

If you forget everything else, remember this: Everyone is a Psychopath.

Nicholas Tharcher
Enroute to Outer Mongolia

---

[25] It should be obvious to every psychopath—and to anyone else with a decent brain—that tyranny and the dark ages are enveloping us at this very moment. Watch your back.

Introduction

Numerous professional editors (i.e., pencils for hire) have refused to assist in the editing of this book. I ask myself why?

Their answer is, that by participating in the publication of this book, they would be helping to "dim the light of civilization." What they really mean is that they are horrified at the prospect of exposing the inherent hypocrisy of most human behavior.

What these professionals seem unable to consider is that the light of civilization is the result of individuals who are capable of inventing light bulbs and turning on the switches. Put another way, all that is best is the result of the aristocracy of spirit which faces the facts and refuses to become confused by the illusion of complexity.

Like any patient in need of an operation, I asked my *surgeons* (editors) to apply all their skill and knowledge toward beautifying this project. But, instead of a healthy excision here and there they have concluded that this book is itself a cancer which must be cut out at all costs. This means that this book can't be beautified—for it is itself the cure of the cancer which pays them.

Of course, if I had labeled this book differently and had been indirect in what I said there would have been no problem. This, then, is the first lesson of this book: *never say exactly what you mean if you want the cooperation of the coward.* No matter how pathetic, everyone is looking out for their best interests. For most people, their best interests consist of not being punished. Few play to win. They play to be safe while feeling morally superior to the winners.

Also, these professionals can't handle, without facing a collapse of their spirit, that you can't improve something that is not designed to be improved—except by radical reconstructive genetic "surgery." You can toss all the money in the world into the pit of the eternal fire of stupidity and all it will do is burn.

University degrees are in disrepute because they deserve to be. Mediocrity reigns. We even lack real people to hate. Lies, deceit and symbols have taken the place of the sword and the gun. Man is a bad animal and worse as a God. What other creature needs holidays to remind him of what to feel and when?

The Christian-Judaic attempt to make a human out of man has failed. What has emerged are two things: 1) The Web Page (but, no matter what one says, the Web is still the home of the Spider) and 2) The Manipulator. He is the fetus who refused to abort.

He is about to happen to you.

There is a lot of slop in life. You can make a ton of mistakes, be the biggest screwup, and still survive—even succeed. Don't let anyone fool you about this. There are millions—billions—of people who believe all kinds of lies and still do well. Some people believe the truth and are utter failures. Life is tolerant, even stupidly so.

What you are about to read is an exposition on how "everything" in the world works. While illustrative and vivid, this small book only touches on the intricacies of the major concepts of control, manipulation and torture which are the major pastimes of mankind.

But I assure you, my dear reader, that "touching" on these subjects may be all you need. You may either feel exhilarated and seek to fill in the blank spaces yourself, or the "touch" of this little book may fill you with such disgust and loathing that you will smash every mirror in your house and pledge to assassinate the author.

Instead of the latter, however, may this small book slowly and directly lead the reader through the workings of the human condition.

Remember, the principles contained herein are applicable to mega-corporations, governments, societies of every kind, families and, of course, you. So read on at your own risk.

The reader should keep in mind that this book is explicit and pulls no punches. Some readers will be very offended by many of the ideas in this book while others will sadly or joyously shake their head in affirmation and seek out the author for personal instruction and guidance. If you do so, be sure to bring a good check.

I wrote this book as a summary of the observations of a well-trained psychologist and social philosopher and, while I am well aware that my personal reputation will suffer in the sterile world of academia, I joyfully make this sacrifice for the honor of sharing my insights and conclusions with hopefully kindred spirits.

As you read this book, keep in mind that you are sharing the secrets of the great "bosses" and kings of all time and, while these secrets might offend you, they *do* control you. So my reader—read well.

The first thing to keep in mind is that nature is not horrible. Almost everyone believes, in one way or another, that nature is malicious; and without human conscience, the world would turn into a nightmare of war, rape, murder, theft, fraud, etc., and that the strong would exploit and destroy the weak.

If such things exist—and they do—they do so with the full consent and sanction of mankind. In fact, this is the *definition* of mankind.

However, there are a few points that we need to get straight. First, the strong will never get rid of the weak as this would yield a poor return on investment. In fact, the strong actually help to breed the weak because, without them, the strong who remained would finally kill each other off.

This would leave the world with but a few individuals separated by vast distances. If this were the case, those remaining would die of boredom.

The common notion that man is a killer is much too narrow. He is simply an exploiter and controller with killing being only one of various possible game outcomes. In other words, all things being equal, like the proverbial cat and mouse, man would rather play with the mouse than kill it—unless, of course, he is starving to death. As long as there are other food sources, it appears that mankind enjoys manipulation and exploitation as its primary species-sport. Man is the ultimate game-player because he pretends that he is not playing a game at all.

Nature is not horrible. Nature is simply nature and the term "horrible" is simply propaganda, created by leaders from the beginning of time to help control the majority of people most of the time.

"Most of the time" is the important phrase because, without some chaos and destruction, the population might wake up to the fact that nature is not inherently horrible; and then who in hell would need leaders to run their lives? Without leaders to complain about, the game would not be fun.

More importantly, for me, without people who deny that they are playing the game of control and exploitation, life could be no fun. One of my favorite games is to make people who believe that they are not playing a control game realize that they are. One of the kicks I get from doing this is watching them suffer from this realization.

It is important to have at least a few people like this in your life. When I feel there aren't enough around me, I make a point of seeking them out and cultivating them.

Without belaboring the point or trying to make the reader feel good, the entire Game of Life is rigged, and even most so-called leaders do not know what is really going on.

This book promotes the idea that the human species, like every other species, has its own favorite sports.

Specifically, the human species loves games which are dominated by control and manipulation, even if they lead to mass destruction—including the destruction of self.

However, part of this game requires that we pretend that we *do* care when, in fact, what we really enjoy is what *leads up* to the spilling of blood. Some people enjoy the blood itself a bit more than others, but I for one would rather call the game quits when I know that I have won.

I am well aware that the position posited in this book will meet with a lot of resistance from the bleeding hearts of the world, but let me give away a little secret right from the beginning: most human beings (the common man) are so numb by their very nature that they are completely unaware that they are playing a major part in this game (albeit as extras) and that, in most instances, the common man doesn't feel an ounce of pain from the process of general exploitation and manipulation.

In other words, the generic victim *needs* to be the victim. He *needs* to be controlled, lest he face a void—an abyss—so deep that Dante himself would have been unable to fill it.

Christopher S. Hyatt, Ph.D.
St. Kitts

Manual I

The Toxick Magician

it is the weak who must tell you they are strong
it is those without love who must make it a law
it is those without will who must tell themselves they have one
it is those who can't shine that need a star
thusly,
the mathematics of the "law" is $\odot=\odot$

1

The willful application and direction of man's mind and power to the ends which he desires is the necessary primal force which accomplishes the true organic will of the Toxick Magician. Often this application will entail doing what normal people call "good," for it is this so-called good-in-itself which, by its very nature, brings about the desired results of the Master: confusion, destruction and the confounding of forces. The Manipulator loves people who do good and, even more so, people who think good thoughts.

Everything which the Establishment and Church desire finally brings about its own ruin and, with it, the establishment of Higher Order(s) of dis-organization—which is the goal of the Master.

An example will serve to illustrate.

The Church's desire to see the end of abortion brings about an inevitable over-population which, in turn, causes the Toxick Chaos necessary to bring about the destruction of the Church and, to a large extent, the environment as we know it. So, send food to Africa!

The Toxick Magician sees all appeals to ecology as futile attempts to maintain stasis. Hence, the preoccupation with ecology leads to a level of destruction far greater than would be otherwise.

For example, consider the cascading effects of water-saving toilets. In order not to clog them, we are now so dis-commoded that we have to shit in segments. People are not able to get rid of their feces as quickly as they used to and this is not safe!!

Consequently, to safeguard their health, people are now buying black-market toilets and installing them illegally under cover of darkness.

The effect of ecology in this case is to create a new criminal underclass and reduce the population through the spread of disease. To cover up the real cause, the blame for the increased mortality rate has been placed on salmonella-infected chickens and tainted red meat, thus eliminating Steak Tartar and Ramos Fizzes from the menus of finer restaurants.

On the positive side, it allows people to become familiar once again with their bodily products, destroys the abomination of Grilled Chicken Caesar Salad, and brings back into vogue scato-divination.

It is worth noting that, if the issue were really the conservation of water, the entire problem could be solved more effectively with a two-button toilet with, of course, the appropriate international icons of yellow drops for number 1 and a brown coil with rising steam for number 2.[26]

The Practitioner constantly looks for small ways to jiggle the environment which will (dis-)attract the attention of the masses. Something as simple as dropping little pieces of paper in the street provides something to do for people with guilt complexes and no meaning in their lives. In a sense, the Manipulator helps reduce the rate of suicide and spouse abuse.

The Master may even choose to help an ecological cause (e.g., the current preoccupation with "flesh eating bacteria") since the stasis brought about by its success will sooner or later lead to a greater displacement and, hence, more Toxicity. Remember, every solution leads to more complex and involuted "problems." The Toxick Magician loves problem-solvers. Better antibiotics make better bacteria!

---

[26] By the time you read this, such toilets may seem old hat. Indeed—except for the icons—we have already seen such toilets in certain parts of the world. Moreover, for years, residents of many water-scarce areas have—somehow—managed to be frugal with this resource without any sort of governmental enforcement whatsoever! (Only the tourists need to be told: "If it's yellow let it mellow; if it's brown flush it down.")

At this point it is worth noting that next week, or next year, or next decade, many of the examples used in this book may seem outdated, old-fashioned, obsolete and/or "quaint." Such is the nature of the evolution of technology. *Nonetheless, the principles of this book are eternal.*

As long as any force and motion is applied, counterforces of the most bizarre and unpredictable types begin to formulate and affect the entire field of play.

The Manipulator knows that we live in gigantic sets of interwoven neucoid-correlation matrices where one tiny push in the right place can cause an entire field to collapse. This might be likened to Kung Fu Magick.

2

The Toxick Magician knows there is no way *not* to create what the Hindu's have called Karma. Karma is good!

He knows this fact very well, and he is also aware that most people live in a superstitious world of "causes and effects."

The Master knows how to take advantage of every superstition because he understands that "causes" as we "know" them also create "effects" as we *can't* know them.

He knows that everyone lives in *bubble(s) of superstition(s)* where magical rewards and punishments lurk and abound. But somewhere in the dark of perceived order there is a monster hiding, ready to devour the "innocent."

He loves to walk down the street in pride and certainty, knowing he's but one moment away from an attack of diarrhea. This makes him unique among the masses. The Toxick Magician always views his adversary with his head in the toilet bowl.

The Practitioner knows, for example, that, if the pro-abortionists win by controlling population, it is the *wrong* population that will be controlled.

This is one of the key principles of Toxick Magick: whether, for example, the Church gets its way or not in terms of abortion is quite irrelevant. *It is the quality and nature of the forces set in motion for which the Toxick Magician strives.*

He knows that whatever is the most gross will triumph in the end. Whatever levels the playing field triumphs for a while.

He knows that the faster technology develops, the greater will be the collisions and destruction within the species which developed the technology. Inertia must always be viewed from the psychological perspective of indolence. Indolence, in one form or another, leads to farce.

Regardless of social strictures, laws or anything else, the masses will continue to breed. The goal is 66.6% *illiteracy* in the Civilized World and not the reverse. The goal of literacy is simply a ruse, a ploy of the Toxick Magician to set into motion those forces which interfere with the natural give and take of intelligence and stupidity, and power and impotency.

Thus, every so-called worthy goal is a ruse and the fuse of destruction. In the end, all goals reduce to control, and the means used to gain control are irrelevant and quickly forgotten.

What difference does it make to the average individual or organization that 10 or 20 million lives are destroyed after a week or two? It is only important that there is a fresh chicken in the pot. This is called "Voodoo Mechanics."

Toxick Magick is the direct application of one's power and abilities to speedily bring about the destruction of mediocrity and stupidity.

However, the Manipulator realizes that what follows is more due to "chance" than direct application. This means that you should not sit around too long thinking about what to do. Set something in motion *now*. Then sit back and watch the fallout.

The natural power behind Toxick Magick is the Hatred of Restriction and the Joy in the power of Freedom and the apparent random application of choice, risk and chaos.

Pain and destruction feed the planet more than pleasure.

A Manipulator's task is to always throw a little something into the works. Learn how to help everyone achieve what they want. It will, in the end, destroy them.

By the perfect application of the mind of a Master, individuals will develop the natural character traits to lead the world into a deep and abysmal darkness until the necessary form of transformed destructiveness occurs, thereby freeing new and more interesting forms to evolve and develop.

For example, as we wind down to ultimate world peace, expect the greatest possibility for a nuclear holocaust.

Note that when speaking of evolution, we use the word "forms" and not "form." The idea of plurality is important in many ways but, for the moment, its importance lies in the fact that multiple users of Toxicity can create competing ends for the yet unborn futures which will create events which will be regarded as beautiful and grotesque.

3

The human mind exists on shifting gradients of superior force and power. The grade of the mind attracts and influences the forces which surround it.

According to the strength of the Practitioner's code of conduct and his willingness to help promote Toxicity and Chaos in the mindset of his neighbor, the appropriate result usually follows: paranoia. The more you can help your neighbor get what he wants, the more his paranoia and anxiety.

Used properly, paranoia is an ideal weapon to create false and misleading struggles which burn the energy of everyone involved. Paranoia is a simple misdirection virus.

We say that paranoia *usually* follows since other Manipulators may be operating in similar areas with different results in mind. But rest assured, all victims live in a world of suspicion and superstition. Thus, paranoia is the *minimum* a good Toxick Magician can expect.

The only major requirement is that all Manipulators know that their ultimate goal is for the good of the gross force field which is forever struggling to give birth to new life forms as quickly as possible, regardless of the cost to the older forms.

Now, at last, the human race has the means to make radical transformations and provide the race with the opportunity to do away with itself in its present dead-end form.

Thus, for example, in order for immortality to exist, most of the human race will need to be destroyed—and it will be.

At first, of course, there will be the obligatory moaning over the "tragedy." But, within a few months, this destruction will be seen as a happy and necessary event, just as euthanasia will, in time, be seen as a "new" solution to the "problems" of over-population and the funding of Social Security systems. (The scenes at the conclusion of Stanley Kubrick's brilliant movie *Dr. Strangelove: Or How I Learned to Stop Worrying and Love the Bomb* present an excellent example of this process.)

Every human, no matter what he tells himself, knows that simply by being alive, he has run into a brick wall in every aspect of his life. This world is a world of in-voluntarism, of Zombies. And the final brick in the wall is involuntary death.

The power of death lies not simply in the cessation of life, but in the reality that death always feels like the "other," and forces most people to feel a distance between their self and their "here-and-nowness." Death is alienation—the final negative outcome.

This is why the housewives of the world are seen everywhere pushing baby carriages and sipping tea as the mushroom clouds form. The Master, on the other hand, always keeps his coffin handy.

Death, which we have been taught can neither be killed, endured nor cured, is the ultimate wound to the self. The Toxick Magician knows otherwise. He knows that once the right forces are in play, death becomes optional.

If he has the mental organization, the active will, and the stamina to exercise his power, he will have immediate control over his adversaries. This allows him to buy time. And isn't buying time our most interesting and perverse activity?

4

Frequently the best way to gain control is through cooperation.

Each and every individual has an almost comical desire to see himself destroyed. This puts an end to the waiting and the filling of time with nonsense. To fill time means to make time tense.

This doesn't argue against the survivalist theory, but in fact is supported by most Neo-Darwinian speculations. This race, in this form, is obsolete. It can't carry the possibilities of the future(s) for too long.

Few individuals can tolerate the mental void of Toxick Chaos which surrounds him. Always there is some little quirk or some little error which causes him some misery, pain or destruction. Without the need to change diapers, most mothers would strangle their infants.

It always appears that this little something or that could have been avoided and, if we didn't wish to hide from the inherent ugliness of the human condition, we could have side-stepped this misery.

But, remember: those who do not readily, eagerly and graciously accept this world of in-voluntarism will be labeled misfits and psychopaths. As such, be prepared—for enemies are needed to blame for every "bad ending."

Look at the dinosaur—they might have blamed the automobile. And if you look at things perversely enough, the death of the automobile might create a species more horrifying than the dinosaur.

Even with horror and death aside, few can tolerate complete success. It leads to boredom and to the final realization that we are all food within the belly of a giant monster whose final goals we only have a glimmer of—and the glimmer we see is not comforting.

Thus, while man doesn't seek death *per se*, he seeks destruction as this provides the opportunity for new and potentially more lively events. Destruction is the great act of control. It is the "no" to in-voluntarism.

The fact that destruction does, in fact, lead to death is purely happenstantial. The organisms of the future will be able to destroy themselves and still continue to live.

Where there exists an innate superiority or power, Toxick Magick will manifest itself.

A good Student will immediately understand this once he realizes that much of what he has called "failure" is truly pre-potent success. This is particularly true when the Student can write his "autobiographies" with complete dispassion. Every autobiography is nothing more than a story of destruction and decay.

Whether a force is ultimately positive or negative doesn't matter, for it sets in motion other forces over which the magician has little or no control.

This form of Chaos is desired since unknown results leads to more Toxicity and Chaos. Toxick Magicians have been called the "Children Who Hate." And, if the truth be known, they do. They hate stupidity, death and restriction. They loathe the idea of linear time.

5

The public in general has no concern as to who is a Manipulator. The public is only concerned with petty criminals who might affect their petty little lives directly. This is why so many white collar criminals go free or get minimal sentences, and why some of the most hideous crimes either go totally unnoticed or are applauded as greatness.

For example, the "great" Hawaiian king, Kamehameha I, is considered "great" because he "unified the islands"—by pushing thousands of his "enemies" off of cliffs.

Similarly, consider the Christian fight against evil in Europe—which was finally victorious when all of the "witches" were burned.

The public concerns itself with the maintenance of its *status quo* (i.e., chickens) and, as a rule, the public should be helped to maintain its *status quo* even more intensely than it is.

The heavier it gets, the deeper it sinks and the greater its fears. It can't succeed or leap to the next level of superiority. It must sink deeper and hold on more strongly.

As it does this, it creates more enemies while, at the same time, making itself more impotent. Do not fight the *status quo* or the failures which surround you. Help it, encourage it, and then help it encapsulate itself. Help it grow stronger and heavier. Use whatever it creates. Don't change it, simply streamline it a little.

Many *normal* magicians regard real power as unattainable. This is natural for them since they do not have any real power to begin with. One who lacks a mind which possesses strength and active processes can't, by its very nature, possess power.

Normal magicians are horrified by the notion of power and control over others. The Toxick Magician has no such terror. What terrifies him is that the *status quo* may gain power over him through his own natural desire to be destroyed and to be replaced by better, more flexible life forms.

Remember, it is a natural tendency to be dark and self-destructive. The trick is to do it well—very well.

Help others get what they want. This is the most insidious form of destroying them. It makes them instantly terminal and, in most cases, useless.

This method is similar to what has been called the Peter Principle. Help each person to reach their highest level of incompetence. Once they are there, they will begin digging in, establish fixed fortifications, and now you have them as a resource—a *tool*, if you would, to do with as you wish.

For example, universities have developed the tenure system to guarantee control over a potentially dangerous and Toxick faculty.

6

Always play to security as if it were an adventure. Always help others think that their attempts to assure themselves security will work. As a Manipulator, we know that most methods to assure security are doomed to fail sooner or later—and fail badly. *It is better to live with danger and chaos than with security.* Your chances of surviving long enough and with enough power are much greater. This is another fundamental principle of Toxick Magick.

There are natural Toxick Magicians and many of my readers know who they are. But there are others who should remain unknown and unknowable, for this affords them the best opportunity to do their work effectively.

These individuals know how to extend their power by being sort of unconscious of what they are doing. Awareness interferes with their activities. One way of recognizing them is from the trails of people they leave behind—people who think they have been helped. In fact, these people have been made into Zombies who later will be used in one way or another to accomplish the desired end of Pandemonium.

The Master is well aware of the value of controlling the psychic powers of others. In other words, what some people believe to be their spiritual, psychic, or higher self is really the shadow spirit of the Master.

It is the will of the Master that is speaking. This result can either be induced or produced in the subject at hand.

Everyone is a potential subject for the Toxick Magician. Each encounter is a laboratory experiment to determine what forces are needed to help the subject develop the correct obsessions and compulsions to accomplish the will of the Practitioner.

He will always first try to bring out what is natural to his victim or tool. This is done, not for moral reasons, but because it conserves energy and time. If this approach doesn't work, then he will simply find other means to produce the effect(s) he wants.

Encounters take place everywhere. This is the beauty of learning how to be an effective Manipulator. All day long, every day, you can inject your will upon others by using their stupidity, their desire to be gullible and, more importantly, their need to be flattered while disbelieving what you say.

People are so fearful of being controlled that this fact in itself makes them prime resources to be controlled.

Every subject will guide you in how you can control them and help them become a slave to aspects of your will. For, although people hate the *thought* of control, most *wish* to be controlled.

Risk, freedom and power are only words for them. Most are simply weak and cowardly, secretly waiting for some superior force to take them over. The proof is self-evident. Just look at the number of people who seek degrees in sociology and education.

The comatose state of ordinary man is necessary, and every attempt to awaken him drives him deeper into security and trance. Thus, every promise to make things better is designed to make him less dangerous and more readily destroyed. Even his revolutions make him into a better slave.

In the process of planetary and intergalactic change there is, of course, the necessity that the Practitioner himself will be consumed by the procedures he uses in reaching his own ends.

He, then, must not counterfeit his real-life experiences into moral platitudes. Once this is done (except as a device for others to believe in), you are no longer dealing with a true Toxick Magician but with someone who is possessed by his beliefs.

Such a person is no longer a real Manipulator; he has become a *True Believer*. This is not to be bemoaned, as True Believers are the very foundation of change. Stagnation always leads to some form of spontaneous combustion. Just look at any garbage heap.

Zombies are a necessary requirement and, the more of them— no matter what the source—is a sign of success.

Many people will reduce all willful action into two simple categories: Black Magick and White Magick. The easiest thing to do with this simple reductionist ploy is to use it to your benefit. In other words, let people call it what they will. Agree with them and help them to firm up their ideas. Help them make their notions so rigid that they can be broken like glass. Other people's stupidity is your resource. Help them to remain stupid.

Remember, one of best ways to get what you want—no matter what it is—is to help other people get what they "whim" they want.

Discord is the politics of mobility.

The more mobile, the more discord you sow. However, it is wise to give the impression of stability and order. This keeps your enemies from controlling *you*.

Remember, the basis of toxicity is control. The more control you have—particularly if people do not know it—the more toxick you are. Some of the most powerful Masters I know appear to be the most obsequious, kind, and helpful people in the world. However, they are the most *dangerous* people in the world— dangerous, that is, to those who believe in the beneficence of man.

7

Do not think that by learning the basic principles of Toxick Magick that a world of ease and bliss will automatically open to you.

The practice of Toxick Magick is hard and the traps are many. One of the worst and most dangerous traps is the "food chain." Every good Manipulator knows exactly where he is on the food chain at any moment in time.

The concept, in and of itself, often separates the real Toxick Magician from the pretenders.

The food chain concept explicitly states that we are in a constant process of consuming each other and being consumed by each other. There are no free lunches and each encounter demands knowledge of who is going to consume whom.

Some people prefer to look upon this as trading: after all, we are human, aren't we? But no, we consume each other all the time, often in subtle ways. Indeed, we live off the flesh and blood of everyone we meet. In fact, right now, each of us is living off the flesh and blood of people we haven't met and others are living off of us.

However, the Practitioner knows how to delve into and apply the most subtle forms of strength or weakness to accomplish his ends.

It is imperative to evaluate what each person wants to consume, the style in which he consumes it, and the utensils he uses. Everyone wants something, even if it is to give away something for "free."

Some people are so overburdened that the greatest way to consume them is to *not* let them help you. By doing this, the Practitioner can create situations in which he can get something from a person that he didn't wish to give.

But beware: You are also food. And knowing how to be consumed (eaten/used) is imperative in your practice. If you are really outclassed, acknowledge this to yourself. If you don't accept the fact gracefully, you will damage yourself severely.

Trying to pull yourself up to your adversary or trying to pull your adversary down to yourself is another common error. This can cause *unnecessary* pain and destruction.

Evaluating the complex and ever-changing positions on the food chain is one the finest applications of your capabilities. Once you have ascended to the position of influence in this area and practice the method to its fullest extent, you will automatically release a vast reservoir of your natural power.

But under no circumstances should you undervalue the power of knowing how to evaluate the power of food-chain consciousness.

Do not be put to sleep by platitudes or niceties. You are always being looked at in terms of use, and use means consumption. Thus, always be prepared to learn new methods of food-chain evaluation. To do this you will have to lose, at least for a while, much more than you will win. One of the secrets in this area is learning how to disguise your scent with marinades.

The Master trusts everyone—that is, he trusts everyone to be human. No matter what disguise each and every person puts on, they are out for their own perception of their best interests—which includes their own self-destruction.

Almost everyone denies that self-destruction is one of their primary goals, but no matter how much they deny it, they practice it. While self-destruction makes way for new—and possibly more interesting—life forms, it also allows people to cope with their feelings of helplessness.

Everyone feels helpless in one way or another. There is no way out of it—except to destroy yourself.

Self-destruction is control, and some control, no matter how painful it might seem, is better than no control at all.

Most so-called insane people are nothing more than bad control junkies. So are most drunks and addicts.

They are very aware of how little control they have except, however, to numb themselves, create artificial delusions of grandeur and, finally, to destroy themselves. And, in the process, cause pain to the world which "refused" them.

This feeling exists only in their own imagination. I have known a number of people who attempted suicide and one of their prime fantasies is watching others cry over them and hate themselves for the way they treated the poor, dead martyr.

If you were there and could have overheard some of these inadequate control junkies, you would have laughed yourself silly. And, frankly, I wouldn't be surprised that some of them, after hearing your laughter, would go right out and try it again.

In the process of understanding the food chain, it is imperative to keep in mind the kind of diet you prefer. Some Toxick Magicians like different types of subjects to manipulate than do others. For example, some like women while others prefer men. (I, for one, like to help women get what they want.)

However, it is imperative to keep in mind that, since Toxick Vampirism is highly sophisticated and intricate, it is important to know that some Practitioners go on particular types of diets before they attempt certain manipulations or activities (e.g., rituals).

Knowing what types of people to "consume" and when to "consume" them can be highly effective in determining the success or failure of a specific venture.

Another way to understand this issue is based on the metaphor of meat-eaters and vegetarians.

Under certain circumstances a meat-eater must go on a vegetarian diet to heal an illness or lose weight. The same holds true with Toxick Magick. Certain psychic diets (which, in this case, means the consumption of the energy of certain types of people), is necessary before embarking on a particular experiment or project.

Eat the psychic food of others which best suits your temperament and the temperament of your operation. If you are going to try a magical operation which requires immense strength, you might try controlling someone you have never controlled before. However, if you fail, you might find that you will need to wait a while before you have enough strength to try again. Be careful not to overindulge or overdo it.

Draining people of energy can sometimes have a rebound effect, particularly if you can't stomach the results. It's like buying a puppy dog and feeling possessed by its following you around all the time. You might have been better off with a cat or a snake. Be careful of what you want, particularly if you do not know how to balance the operation.

The balance of any operation counts on the mixture of ingredients which goes into making up the whole meal. And, for some people, looking at a ritual as if it were the preparation of a fine meal is an excellent device to guarantee a successful operation.

Sometimes a meal which appears out of balance (such as an all meat diet), may be the exact thing for the forces which you plan to deal with. Sometimes alcohol or other substances can backfire on a operation which requires focused, conscious thought, while at other times alcohol may be exactly the right ingredient to make the operation a success.

Regardless of what you decide to "eat," both psychically and physically, normally overindulgence will not prove to be useful. In fact, few operations which concern money, sex, or power benefit from overindulgence.

If you feel that overindulgence is necessary, wait until the operation is completed. The higher powers and forces sometimes appreciate a great feast afterwards both to signify your commitment to them and to feed a particular entity.

This issue brings up a very important point. You must reward entities which assist you and punish entities which either harm or interfere with your work.

When you are evaluating someone on the food chain, it is important to take into account the quality of their brain and the beauty or ugliness of their body.

Extracting energy from dull-witted or very ugly people, while still energy, can cause psychic indigestion. This idea follows from the old axiom: "Be careful who you hang out with, you might become like them."

This fact is often ignored, not only in the simple day-to-day operations between people, but in the area of Toxick Magick. Although a Master can normally offset this effect, most apprentices are not yet strong enough to accomplish this, particularly if they are surrounded by parasites and defeatists.

Under these conditions, it is best to stay away from these people, especially if there are too many of them gathered in a single place. On the other hand, if there are a few, simply take control of them.

Do not allow them to influence you. Build a shield around them first and, if that doesn't work, get away. But don't build a constant shield around yourself because it might inhibit other work which you might be doing. Personal shield building is only necessary under certain conditions.

Since the power of the Practitioner is a function of both natural superiority and intense practice, it is important to choose the right times and places for practice, as well as the right victims for your operations.

8

As more people find that they are innately Toxick, some competition will tend to break out among practitioners. This is natural since, at this time in our history, more people are being born with the talent of manipulating darkness and participating in the destruction of normal humans.

I often feel overjoyed when I find out that some worn-out impediment to our futures—and the futures of the developing life forms—has been destroyed, or has become so rigid that its own operating system is failing.

For example, consider the effects of ever-increasing over-population. For normal people this is a worry because of the drain of resources. For the Toxick Magician it is a joy, *particularly* because it is a drain of resources.

He scoffs at such notions or problems. Every problem is simply an opportunity to fuel the feeding frenzy.

Groups that hate each other and wish to destroy each other are simply tools for the Manipulator.

For example, the periodic "Satanic Scares," witch hunts over organized child abuse, and all TV media-events are viewed first as jokes and then as proof that this particular species has reached the end of its utility.

The species is simply a resource for the latent, hidden viruses of this planet—much as *this* planet may be a resource for another planet.

The entire process is a food chain which the Master actively supports and utilizes for his comfort and fun. He knows that everything is part of the problem and that there are no solutions from a conventional point of view. He knows that millions die daily and millions are born to take their place. He knows that the planet is alive as a stomach is alive—it digests everything.

The Manipulator always contributes to the problem—even when he gives millions of dollars to charity. He knows that each mini-solution will lead to a greater and bigger problem in the long run. He knows that a vaccine which will save lives will, in the long run, actually destroy more lives or let the wrong people die and the wrong people live.

Few people have the strength and fortitude to stare directly into the eyes of the future forms which are preparing to take our place. Few can stand the face of the superman. Few can bear the horrors that await and no one can stop them. Every law enacted is just another nail in the coffin, and to watch the True Believer suffer and be tortured is a great joy. It feeds you.

It is important to have a number of separate, independent, and different food sources to feed and maintain you, depending on your ever-changing needs.

For example, I engage in "friendships" and dialogues with people who normally would hate each other, but who I use for sustenance and enthusiasm.

Both Satanic cults and Christian fundamentalists are closer to seeing the truth than most normal people.

Something is going on, but it's not what they think. The Beast is staring out from each pair of eyes you see. Each glance in the mirror is the story of this world—and the Toxick Magician loves mirrors. Each time he sees his face, he sees the self-destroying power of the species and the planet. This is his true freedom, which transcends any cult and any cult hero.

He knows that each person suffers silently and secretly and each person is constantly making up stories to hide his own hideousness from himself and others.

He has the strength and fortitude to face the Void and see the Beast deep within, eating its way out.

He knows that flesh is mostly for pain—that pleasure is more fleeting and pain is more enduring. He laughs into the Cosmic Belly of Hell as the Beast consumes him

Every time people have children the Toxick Magician is overjoyed, for he knows that within this little bundle is suffering, death and destruction. He is overjoyed with hope that each little bundle contains the seed of the next monster.

9

Every human life form is totally and completely occupied with itself.

Even if you appear to be the center of someone else's activities, it is still the person and his preoccupations which are the real center. Never forget this, no matter how interested someone seems in you.

They are interested in how you fit—or might fit—into their food chain. Never be fooled by people who sacrifice themselves for you. Without their so-called sacrifice, they would be isolated, depressed or feel utter emptiness.

Self-sacrifice is an addiction. Self-sacrificers are often closet- or ex-morphine addicts. I can't tell you how many addictions are prevented and/or "cured" through substitution. The number would certainly be startling to most people.

The idea of "for someone else's good" is patently absurd, even if the victim receives benefit. People constantly confuse results with motive, and it is much more comforting to ascribe mystical and altruistic motivations to events than to accept them as magical acts of will (the Merlin phenomenon), or random consequences of complex interaction neucoid-correlation matrices.

If you place twelve people together in a room, certain unpredictable outcomes have to occur. This is true even if you limit the interests of the dozen to preparing and sharing food.

Every human, while occupied with himself, desires to get away from himself and play "follow the leader." Follow the leader is not always noticeable in every area of a person's life, but the desire to follow must express itself somewhere in a person's life.

Masters have learned how to use this instinct in themselves and in others.

They can imitate others and reflect those qualities which the person loves and admires in himself. The expert can always spot the areas in which a person wants to follow or be dependent. Once this information is properly assimilated into the Toxick Magician's neucoid-correlation matrix, the Magician begins to close in.

He becomes more capable than ever of consuming the energies and resources of that person. So, if you are strong enough, remember that no one really likes you. What they like is how you make them feel, and how well you fit into their resource scheme.

If a Manipulator does something for someone, he never allows himself to be totally repaid. He always wants an edge. However, he always allows his victim to repay him to a certain degree lest the victim turn into a enemy.

People are always keeping count of what they owe and what is owed to them. Few people are capable of simply taking without its finally having a devastating effect on their personality. However, there are some who are expert at it.

I personally know of three, but even in these cases there are occasional paybacks which seem to have a random quality. None of these three are Toxick Magicians. In fact, they are excellent examples of altruists and martyrs who mostly sneak their pleasures behind closed doors and always at the expense of everyone they know—while, all the time, claiming innocence and ignorance.

One of these even chastises himself for not understanding the ways of the world while he insidiously manipulates everyone to conform to his views and to give him what he wants.

But he is not a Toxick Magician. He doesn't help people destroy themselves by helping them get what they want, nor is he concerned with advancing himself in any real-world terms. He lives totally in his imagination, and is an ideal victim for any good Practitioner. I have been utilizing his energy for years and he is still going strong.

Do not forget that helpful behavior is often nothing more than the attempt to build points for future security. While it might be *natural* for such a person to give, at the same time he is giving he is also accumulating points which, sooner or later, will be collected.

The collection process can even be displaced—that is, collected from someone who doesn't owe that person a thing. This is often caused by frustration which leads to depression or aggression. Neither state can be tolerated for too long, so the results of the frustration build and find release in sado-masochistic activities—which include extracting points from any victim.

Note that I didn't say *innocent* victim, for no one alive is innocent. Everyone is involved in accumulating points and surviving. Thus, every act of survival is an act of destruction. Every breath destroys universes. We are all murderers.

These sado-masochistic acts include punishments dealt out both upon others and upon oneself. But even if a person simply punishes himself, his pitiful sight is punishment for all those around him.

If he wishes to be helpful, his best bet is to commit suicide—unless, of course, he learns how to be a Toxick Magician and uses his natural self-destructive habits in a more effective and satisfying fashion.

If you ever have to use force to get what you want, be prepared for anything. Unless you are completely assured that you can destroy the other person completely and with impunity, do not use physical force or the threat of physical force to get what you want. Even if you receive what you want, you will have made a potential enemy.

There are exceptions. The threat of force may be necessary from time to time with certain schizoid, masochistic types who feel highly anxious unless they feel completely controlled. It will even be necessary to use actual force from time to time to keep such a person from going off the deep end. In this sense you might consider yourself a lifesaver.

10

The disparity coefficient between Toxick Magicians and regular people is enormous, and this disparity is easily observable even among Practitioners.

The disparity coefficient is a number derived by complex mathematics which tells us the difference between how a person lives (observed behavior) and how he *ought* to live if he wishes to benefit himself and the planet as a whole. Thus, the disparity coefficient can tell us whether or not someone *is* a Toxick Magician, and then tell us how good a Practitioner he is.

A good Manipulator is like a farmer with many fields. At any time he is in various stages of planting, reaping, sowing, and allowing the land to rest. This is a very important model—although some prefer the hunter-gather model. I, for one, use and combine both. To be a stalker and a gatherer and a farmer is, in my view, an ideal formula for proper operation. Unfortunately, however, I learned some of my skills too late in life to take full benefit of them.

As is so often said by psychologists and philosophers, humans go through a protracted period of "maturation" when compared to other species. This lengthy period of being a child and under the thumb of various authorities makes the human a prime candidate for re-instituting the infantilizing process during *any* period of his life.

For example, consider most people's response to the Toxick Platitude: "Everything I Needed to Know I Learned in Kindergarten." They nod their head knowingly and smile because an authority has endorsed as brilliance what they had always thought was shame.

Most forms of learning, teaching and punishment are nothing more than forcing infantile and childish roles upon others.

Most of the modern health profession is pervaded by this technique of infantilizing the "patient." It is especially common among physicians, dentists and psychotherapists.

The most adept of these might be called "terrorist doctors." They are commonly found, for example, among the majority of gynecologists (who get a thrill from terrorizing women into signing off on unnecessary hysterectomies) and cardiologists who routinely stampede their victims into unnecessary, useless and dangerous invasive procedures which "must be done immediately or you could die at any moment." (This latter group has been so successful that the "zipper," which characterizes open-heart surgery, has become a status symbol.)

Most psychotherapists, of course, have always treated their "patients" as infants. As the field has driven out the few good therapists in favor of the mediocrity of the "housewife therapist," the opportunity for infantilization has expanded dramatically. Witness the self-righteousness, witch-hunt mentality of "adult survivors of child abuse" and the stylishness of Multiple Personality Disorder.

One of the key factors in understanding why people are so pathetic is that, during the infantile stage of development, they "come to constant erroneous conclusions" as to "what causes what."

In other words, they learn erroneous negotiation strategies right from the very beginning and come up with conclusions about themselves, the world, and their interconnections which they continue to use and be victims of until they are buried alive.

The reason they survive at all is because of "slop" (i.e., most people have the same wrong conclusions).

Building upon wrong conclusions leads to habits which, once ingrained, are difficult if not impossible to break. People's minds become calcified. They blindly proceed through their lives, deceiving themselves and repressing the immense spite they have accumulated over all the years for continuously being treated like children.

If this is not bad enough, all humans have a collection of traumas and have learned to carry around a backpack of anxieties.

I have often said of the human that he suffers from an auto-immune disease. He desires oblivion while, at the same time, loathing the idea of losing control and his occasional feelings of integrity.

He can't tolerate his condition, but has no way out short of self-destruction. For man, life is a blind assembly line. Each person thinks he is free while secretly living out the fantasies of his DNA.

His needs and resentments are so intense that annihilation through symbolic means is often his only option. He can't flee and he sees no one in particular to fight. Thus the need for symbolic substitutions such as masochism, depression, war, enemies, and so forth.

For example, there are wars on drugs, fruit flies, border invasions ("illegal aliens") and even the occasional revolution.

There is no therapy for the human condition as death, decay, disease, detention, and dementia always force themselves on this pitiful creature in one form or another.

One solution to man's pitiful condition of dependency and vulnerability is *narcissism.*

Buried somewhere in every person are delusions of grandiosity and perfection and a desire to be admired. Although the direct expression of these feelings is not allowed (except through acceptable means), they are the basis by which the human being survives his dead-end condition.

No matter what happens, each person holds on to these delusions; without them he would die. The Toxick Magician is quite aware of these complex dynamics and uses them for all they're worth.

All governments (some might assert that I should have said "authoritarian" governments, but this is, in fact, a redundant notion) count on "their" "citizens" to respond in typical infantile fashion. This includes identifying unconsciously with a more powerful force, even if this force enslaves, brutalizes and humiliates you. For most people, slavery *is* freedom.

Thus, democracy is nothing but a ruse to hide the power and force of this technique. Adolph Hitler was an expert in its use. He knew that the German People wanted to be children with a strong magical father to care for them. However, the German people, like any other group of people, would have felt offended if their nose was rubbed in what they had to become in order to get what they believed they wanted.

The chronic process of making—and being made—the child is a technique at which every bureaucrat and government official is adept. This is fundamentally how the police operate. The Master is an expert in this area.

This is particularly true when others attempt to make the Master Practitioner into a child. He knows how to let others think they are accomplishing their ends and, as they relax and expose themselves, the Master can strike—if he so chooses.

However, more often than not, the Toxick Magician will save the information he has gained by letting others make him into a child and then use it at the most appropriate times.

The method of reducing everyone to a child is primary for this species and pervades this planet. All life forms have the means to turn every situation into a potentially "infantilizing" one.

The Toxick Magician is conscious that a boomerang effect can occur when someone is made aware that they have to play a childlike role in order to get what they want.

Unlike most people, the Manipulator knows how *not* to use his authority to excess. No act of intimidation is free of a price and the price for playing on the needs of adults to be children can be two-fold—sabotage and dependence. Often, both occur at the same time.

The Practitioner is well aware of what types of people will respond with what reaction. Sabotage is the most common method. Often this takes the form of passive-aggressive behavior. We note this often in the American factory when workers sabotage the company's profit because they resent the role of being told what to do. The worker, of course, carries this home to his family where he has the opportunity to brutalize his wife and she has the opportunity to brutalize the children and the children have the opportunity to brutalize the pets. This is the essence of the nuclear family.

The entire structure of the world is a food chain of infantilizing. Everyone gets to play adult and child in various situations and many people relish any minor role of authority so they can get even.

One way to counteract rebellious employees is to give them the opportunity to infantilize someone else or to act in some role of authority. At one time, suggestion boxes served this function. However, employers must continually come up with other techniques because employees have a way of finding out how seriously they are taken.

Most people perform so poorly in the role of adult that they rarely get complete satisfaction from this process. They are so contaminated by their infantile roles that they overreact or underreact in the role of authority. The Toxick Magician is well aware of these failures and is aptly capable of taking advantage of them.

Normal people search out situations where they can be the king. This includes cultivating hobbies, developing special talents or useless knowledge, pursuing addictions, being the angry or bitchy shopper or the irate tenant or the bossy or cranky eater, joining political groups, developing severe psychological symptoms, and other normative activities.

Some people are so desperate to be the King that they allow themselves to be severely tortured and humiliated. Even when they are on their knees, in their mind they believe they are controlling the person who is hurting them and this is what ultimately provides them with satisfaction. Other types have learned how to yell and throw adult temper tantrums to make others feel small and childlike. The Practitioner should know how to handle each of these situations to his satisfaction.

11

One technique that the Toxick Magician uses is making something look harder than it is.

Universities constantly use this ploy and the longer people live the more difficult things will have to be made. So, instead of taking three years to learn a skill which should have only taken one year, it will now take five years.

Making things look harder and taking more time allows for better indoctrination and control of the victim who wishes to have a better life for himself by getting the sanction of certain groups.

Most people want to be Certified by someone greater than themselves. The idea of having a life without some form of Certificate will become more and more terrifying as the beast becomes more complex and begins to fall apart. This is when the Manipulator begins to shine. He is always best at—"fall apart."

The Practitioner knows how to hold out the Right Carrot and to create just the right amount of difficulty and humiliation to make an ally out of a potential enemy.

He knows how to get the victim to identify with his causes and his needs and to make him grateful for all the misery he has been caused.

The victim now becomes a True Believer as the Toxick Magician manipulates the parameters of fear, failure, reward, punishment and success in just the right fashion.

He knows that people have no direct access to truth, nor do they have the ability to find out what truth is.

Instead they have religions, superstitions, degrees, certificates, test scores, badges, passports, licenses, and, of course, good old-fashioned ancestor worship.

These all have in common the worship of authority and power which the common man attempts to manipulate through gestures (i.e., obsessions), hopes, beliefs and structured living.

For example, she gets her college degree; gets married (which, in turn, unrolls an entire subset of additional obsessions such as making babies, attending school functions, arranging baptisms, buying houses, and selecting furniture); getting a job (which provides its own subset of obsessions such as buying a car, being preoccupied with taxes, looking forward to holidays and vacations, attending office parties, working to improve social status, preparing for retirement); retirement (which brings preoccupation with diseases, leisure, and grandchildren); and—finally—death.

The truly funny thing about all of this is that *each and every person* thinks that he is deciding and controlling these activities intentionally and consciously and that they are *unique in the history of the world.*

In reality, anyone with an ounce of awareness knows that these activities are common, banal, trite, vacuous, insignificant, boring and ridiculous—and make for great sport for the Manipulator.

He will often make believe that he takes these things seriously as he disrupts these "unique" social patterns.

For example, he can have a good laugh over someone's mother having her varicose veins stripped or John's getting caught having an affair or Bill's having been diagnosed with manic-depressive psychosis.

The normal man can be defined by his repetitive routines. He takes vacations every year—some even take them at the same place every year. He performs certain behaviors and avoids others on certain days of the week. Humans only have a small set of events to look forward to. How many Christmases can you tolerate!!

If a man sat alone, bought nothing, did nothing but had the physical strength to act, he would either destroy himself or everything about him. The fact that we measure time linearly while, at the same time, the days repeat endlessly until we die, attests to the reality of the human condition.

Even the normal man knows, at some level, that all of this is meaningless and empty. Some even respond to this condition by having a nervous breakdown. The cure, however, is fascinating: few psychologists or psychiatrists would propose that the patient climb Mt. Everest, sail across an ocean, quit his job, divorce his wife or abandon his children.

Instead almost all of them will provide the drug-of-the-moment and help the poor schnook return to the very routines which drove him mad to begin with.

Understanding this is an incredibly powerful opportunity for the advanced Toxick Magician.

12

While human life appears intricate and human activity numerous for the average man, quite the opposite is true. The Toxick Magician knows how to clarify the habits and willingness of his victim in order to get him to respond to his own basic desires.

He knows how to raise every need and desire to just the right pitch, making the victim more susceptible—even *eager*—to embrace his will. Each person is simply an instrument that the Manipulator plays.

In addition, every Master knows how to mis-direct his activities and use the mis-directions of his victim.

Every victim has numerous explanations to make beautiful and individual his automated and fearful behaviors. Every victim has platitudes and moralisms to hide his greed, envy and jealousy. And every victim has a morass of rationalizations and denial mechanisms to mask the numerous sins that keep him living in perpetual shame and guilt. Thus, the Toxick Magician knows that each person is already well-controlled (habituated and ritualized) and all that is needed is the right push here or there to create the desired effect.

Every human is a heap of convictions which he uses to assure himself that he exists as a "real" "individual." In fact, this heap of convictions is the entire content of this bag of flesh called the common man, particularly when it is in the presence of others. He babbles on, spouting a fetid, green slime of nonsense syllables which constitute all that he "thinks" and "values" about what should be and what shouldn't be.

The victim's first goal is to impress upon others his boundaries of individuality on which, if someone happens to trespass, unpleasant consequences might ensue. This is simply the posturing of the insecure whose convictions are nothing more than platitudes and "divine" revelations indoctrinated during childhood.

The Manipulator has no need to express his convictions—unless it serves his purpose to control and create effects.

For example, he might express the opinion that he doesn't "believe in welfare" while all the time letting others know how much he gives to charity. Doing this allows others to think they have discovered who someone "really is" (i.e., how they really work). Letting others discover who they think you are is much better than telling them. People tend to intensively believe what they find out for themselves, particularly if they think you have been hiding something from them.

The Toxick Magician is well aware how important it is to let others discover things for themselves. He accomplishes this by leaving clues and establishing puzzles and simple contradictions which others can easily solve for themselves.

He knows that each person is a detective, albeit a bad one, but a detective nonetheless. As people get to know one another, "great discoveries" by the victim dispel the distrust everyone fundamentally feels toward each other.

Subtly or unconsciously each person knows he is playing a role. Thus, discovering the "truth" for himself helps the person give the Manipulator more control than intended.

It is important to be aware that, secretly, everyone wants to be controlled—but in a way which is acceptable to them. Everyone wants to give away what they have—along with all the associated responsibility—as long as it is done in a way which appears respectable to them. After all, they must keep their illusion of pride—which consists of fearfulness and willfulness. These two factors are often combined in ways that make people appear more complex than they really are.

People are *not* complex and the good Toxick Magician keeps this in mind, while at the same time giving the opposite impression to everyone he engages. He makes everyone feel unique and complex and pretends to take their troubles to heart.

The more the Practitioner hangs out with the common people, the more he understands the cues which they use to make decisions of trust and their willingness to surrender control. Remember, to be in control is frequently painful for most people.

This requires that the Manipulator hang out with groups from various social strata in order to learn their cues. This may even mean lowering oneself to a level which normally would be unacceptable. In fact, doing this from time to time is good training, and giving charity and alms to those one finds the most disgusting is a very good technique for building the necessary character to deal with more powerful and dangerous encounters which are sure to occur in an active career.

13

The Toxick Magician understands how pride works. He knows that if people are forced to lower themselves *unwillingly,* there will be hell to pay at a later date.

Some people thrive on making people lower themselves and giving in. In fact, making people give in is good practice for what *not* to do. Help people decide for themselves to help themselves by giving in to you. This is the most subtle and powerful form of control. Always first help people to help themselves. If this doesn't work, more aggressive steps are necessary. However, even at the last moment, be mean in a good spirit. Always show a sense of good spirit no matter what you are doing.

For practice, it can be useful to push people's convictions to the breaking point. If you attempt this experiment, be sure a good rapport has been developed between you and the victim. Be sure a good flow of energy has been induced and you have the strength and the vigor to control yourself from making unnecessary emotional outbursts. Remember, your goal is to get the victim to lose control over the irrationality or stupidity of his belief.

Before performing this activity, however, first take dancing lessons. Dancing through the mind of a person is very similar to dancing with your feet. If you can't take lessons, go to places where people dance and learn to watch them.

Also learn to watch people while they are drunk. In fact, it is a good idea to get drunk yourself at least once a month. This will give you the opportunity to see how much you are improving in self-control.

When helping people to lose control, learn how to help them save face. Saving face is very important. I suggest learning this habit by almost bringing a person to their knees, and then giving them a reprieve.

For example, if you gain a minor concession from someone, appear to reconsider what they said for a moment or two, and then tell them that they have a good point. However, remember that you have raised their level of arousal and tension and this

---

may be an opportune time to get them to give in to another issue which has nothing to do with your present situation.

It is extremely important to know how to manipulate another person's tension level and, as with many things, timing is everything. Learning how to approach people when they are unduly tense or relaxed is an excellent way to get what you want.

14

The picture of the human condition and the Toxick Magician's means and methods for manipulating it to his ends may not sound romantic to many. Eexcept, of course, to the Toxick Magician, whose sole purpose is to explore, exploit and control the conditions of life.

The fact that he attempts to turn the mundane into an adventure is his primary badge of honor. If a normal person reads this material or tries the methods described herein, instead of a badge of honor he will be wearing a badge of horror.

The power and force of the influence of the Practitioner can be augmented in various ways. First and foremost, practice makes perfect. This implies that there will be many so-called "failures" which provide the necessary lessons for how to present and preserve oneself during a failure.

Another way of increasing power is through alignment with other Manipulators who have similar aims and goals.

It is also sometimes useful to help another Toxick Magician accomplish his own particular end even if you do not directly benefit from it. In these conditions, you will have the opportunity to observe, from a different angle, the operations of another Practitioner (and perhaps even of a Master!).

Third, it is also useful from time to time to surround yourself with many disciples from whom you can drain resources and energy.

This tactic is especially fun if you know the dynamics among the people in your group. If you know each of their vulnerabilities and strengths and how the other members play them, you can drain off greater power which you will need when you find yourself in extreme and dangerous circumstances. And do not doubt it, you *will* find yourself in extreme and dangerous circumstances from time and time and you will need every trick in the book to win—or even to survive.

As you practice "failure" and note your own reactions (particularly feelings of smallness and humiliation), you will begin to find ways of turning these feelings into healthy and free reactions. You will also learn how to use these reactions to cause severe pain in your adversaries. Remember, some adversaries will also try to reverse your power and escape from your control. The means which they use to accomplish this will give you deeper insight into their needs and most secret desires.

Once you sense that you have gained an insight into their secrets, offer them some aspect of it in a way which will not offend them or make them look small. Once they accept your offer they are yours—unless, of course, they too are true Toxick Magicians. If this is the case, back off until you find out more or make a psychological alliance.

15

So far, the objective of practicing Toxick Magick is to provide relief from life for your subject, thereby assuring yourself adventure and resources.

The more often you can relieve people from responsibility in a way they can accept, the more likely they will allow you to drain them. Often they will come directly to you for draining or punishment.

These are often opportune times to refuse them. This allows you to build confidence in yourself and a greater sense of slavery in your victim.

Fail them from time to time. Make them work harder, even humiliate themselves in some fashion, and then show them some respect and love. Sooner rather than later they will be eating out of your hand.

Remember, always be sure to give relief at some time. Allowing tension to remain for too long a period of time can damage your resource. Relief, even if it comes through humiliation, is welcomed.

It is important to reinforce the idea that the Toxick Magician is not the cause of human suffering. *Human suffering is the norm.* Being numb to the depth of this suffering is normal. Being unaware of the stupidity of life is a necessary defense for the survival of this particular species.

The Manipulator is fully aware that anyone who accepts and adapts to this stupidity is not a member of the futures to come and is nothing more than a breeding machine for more slaves.

The Practitioner didn't invent the human condition. He is only taking advantage of it by helping others get what they want. The human condition is simply slavery—a repetition of species behavior from one generation to the next. The difference between humans and other organisms is that there are appear to be more wild card possibilities—and this includes the complete annihilation of the species.

The Toxick Magician accepts these fundamentals and doesn't lament. Instead he helps the species to replace itself with something better, something more flexible, something stronger, something immortal.

This will require the death of billions of people and/or the leaving of this particular planet. Whatever it takes, the Practitioner is constantly preparing himself both in attitude and information. However, he is not fooled—like some—by man's inventions or or by man's cleverness in certain areas.

He is completely aware that man uses all of his inventions to further his primitive nature, and to wait for evolution to catch up is pure folly.

He attempts to force life to speed up the process of evolution—even if it costs him his own life—but he only does this out of choice.

Toxick Magick is *focused* magic, and the Toxick Magician saturates the wound called mankind with his own vitality.

He obtains this vitality by consuming the energy which others are more than willing to "give" away. They don't want it—it is too much for them and the Manipulator knows just the right means for gathering in this "food" and digesting it. He knows just the right temperature to store it and, best of all, he knows just how to prepare it, to make it a joyous and delightful meal.

He knows that the easiest method for gathering in this energy is to help people continue to delude themselves, to help them get what they think they want.

16

Every once in a while, a Toxick Magician will run across someone who is somewhat aware of the truths of human existence. If this person has the fortitude and the willingness, the Practitioner can help this person to himself become a Toxick Magician.

This is a particularly problematical exercise and commitment, and is fraught with dangers and difficulties. This exercise should only be taken on after deep deliberation and testing of the subject. It is imperative that the subject be tested in numerous ways.

It is best if the subject is attractive in some sense, has some charisma and has an above average IQ. Having some special talent is also a good indication that the Manipulator's time will not be wasted.

But these are only preliminaries. Numerous tests must be passed and many skills learned before the Practitioner can be assured that his subject is worthy.

However, it is also very important to keep in mind the idea of circles within circles. Everyone is of some use, especially those who hate the Toxick Magician. Everyone can't become a member of the inner circle, and there is no harm in having many grades of practitioners.

17

The stronger and more knowledgeable the Toxick Magician, the greater the tasks he can successfully complete.

For example, he is aware that he can stir people to chaotic behavior by convincing them that they are getting less than what they are used to. He is also aware that by stimulating people to do more and more, while giving them nothing, can lead them into states of depression and hopelessness. Also, he is acutely aware of the danger of hope in situations which have been very oppressive.

He uses these devices (among many others), to help people get what they really want: more for less.

He pretends that he respects the rights of people and is interested in their plights. Even though most people know that this is a ruse, they go along with the program because it is the line of least resistance and allows them to express some of their frustrations. This reduces the pain of their pent-up depression and aggression.

As a rule, people believe they have honor and a reputation to protect and the Practitioner can manipulate their reactions by casting doubt on their honor or reputation. This can be done by either supporting or threatening them. Often, casting doubt by the method of support has the most useful benefits.

The Manipulator is always aware how much self-delusion is taking place when he is engaged in any conversation. He either helps the self-delusion along to the point that no one believes anyone any longer—thus ending the conversation by switching the topic—or enhances the self-delusion just enough to inflate the person's public value.

People can't help but exaggerate their importance, even if it means that they only exaggerate it to themselves. At the same time, their self-importance is so fragile that the Toxick Magician must be aware of what activities or attitudes might deflate the potential victim.

The Manipulator is always ready to make some form of restitution for a perceived wrongdoing. Often a small apology is enough. At this point, it is often useful to talk about other people in a derogatory or gossipy manner.

Give the victim the sense that you are taking him into your "strictest confidence." Although there is some likelihood that you might not be fully believed, if the person about whom you are gossiping is in some way competitive with your victim, you will be *doubly* believed.

Any type of gossip establishes bonds and, secondarily, alerts others that they, too, might be betrayed at a later date. Thus, the Practitioner always uses gossip wisely. Often he will let the other person do the gossiping while keeping his mouth shut. Or he might say something which will be heard as gossip by his victim, but which also has a double meaning which he can easily twist around if later confronted.

He is expert at lying and confounding information. Little slips and small distortions make for potentially great future power plays which, if well orchestrated, will produce excellent results.

18

While people scream about the importance of social justice, it interests them little unless they are in some way harmed. In fact, the idea of social justice is something about which almost everyone is frightened.

For most people, social justice would mean ruin since almost everyone has lied, stolen, distorted the truth, harmed others in insidious ways, and held back favors out of selfishness, greed, or simple meanness. Thus, from time to time, someone must be sacrificed to atone for and hide the sins of the group or even an individual.

In cases like this, the Toxick Magician can perform miracles. He can help any group, no matter how small, to find a victim to blame and torment.

By relieving the group of blame, he will often find them willing to provide small favors which he should take as soon as they are offered. In some instances, delaying the acceptance of a gift is the best thing to do, but not in the case of scapegoating. People want to forget this petty part of themselves as quickly as possible.

If you do a favor for someone who sees himself as honorable and reputable, be sure to get paid well in advance. These people have a very short memory when it comes to being associated with someone who might make them look bad in the future.

The Practitioner is well aware that all people like to use reason and logic to help them follow and fulfill their whims. In practical terms, this means talking in moderation while always promising a miracle.

Since most people have been in a chronic state of hypnotic trance since childhood, it takes very little to keep them asleep. Thus, it is ideal to promise miracles which are associated with stimuli which remind them to forget the promise when the miracle fails to appear in the form expected.

Miracles will *always* appear in unexpected ways—which you can take credit for.

Of course, having a scapegoat is another means for dealing with failed miracles. Still another method is to mention that no miracle will occur and that more effort or hard work is needed for the desired results.

But no matter what you do, a miracle is always expected. This fact is based on a number of "natural laws," the first of which is that no one has experienced their own creation, and life goes on no matter what happens.

All of this, and more, seems like miracles for which the Toxick Magician knows how to take credit.

It is easy to be a miracle worker. Just allow the obvious to happen. Since most people are in an hypnotic trance, if you can just see 10% of the obvious you are a miracle worker. If you can see 25%, you are a God.

People will always associate whatever precedes an event as the *cause* of the event. As such, always let your presence precede a happy occurrence and always let someone else precede a painful one.

19

The Toxick Magician is well aware of the constant battle between aspects of the same force: the desire for complete control and the desire for the unpredictable—which brings about the necessary destabilization of the entire human structure.

As the desire for predictability (control) increases, natural consequences are automatically set in motion which lead to destabilization or Chaos.

This process happens both cosmically and microscopically. This theory doesn't assume a simple linear process within this gigantic struggle, but instead assumes *multiple* processes (which, from time to time, might include a simple linear process).

In other words, the mathematical functions are multiple, and are sometimes interactive and complex. This leads to inconsistent error when certain phenomena are scrutinized, since stabilization and destabilization are forever interacting, and something may be on the verge of complete destruction (metamorphosis) while appearing completely stable at the moment of observation.

Humans are control freaks. The Manipulator knows that, even stronger than the *reality* of sex and food, is the desire *to control* sex and food.

Once something comes under apparent control, the organism seeks to control other events to the extent that it invents games and devices which provide the opportunity to play the control game.

The Practitioner spends a good deal of time analyzing the peculiar way(s) in which people play their control game(s).

The desire to control is so powerful that suicide and mass madness are sometimes the only things which will satisfy this desire.

At other times, on a more individual level, people will force a collapse of personality so they can begin controlling small things —like "not drinking for the next minute"—to get the high of being in control.

Sometimes control junkies are so involuted and play such strange control games that it appears that control is the *last* thing they desire. In fact, this is not the case.

Control is what they desire, even if they have to force someone else to take up the cause for them. The Toxick Magician is an expert in helping people stabilize and de-stabilize. He knows just when to introject the necessary force to accomplish his end—which is, of course, control.

He helps people seek destruction and death to escape the tension of living. For most people, time is tension and the clock, with its tight spring "forever unwinding," is an ideal model. The tension unwinds until the clock stops.

The Manipulator knows how to hold out hope. Hope allows the food on the chain the illusion that time has not run out. However, hope can't be used continuously. Reality is just too much. Aging, death, pain, loss and fear are just too real and, sooner or later, the spring doesn't wish to be wound up again. But, in spite of this wish, the Toxick Magician may give it a wind or two anyway.

Hope springs eternal and, just as the hope is coming to fruition, it is swallowed up by the monster of time.

The Practitioner doesn't believe in the progress of human nature, nor does he believe in the progress of human behavior. The Toxick Magician operates on the premise that most people seek conflict, both internal and external, to the degree they can tolerate.

Since most humans can't tolerate too much inner conflict (tension)—as it makes them too aware of time—they seek external causes and events to occupy themselves. Thus, *status quo* is always defined in terms of the level and type of conflict and tension a person can tolerate.

For example, I met one man who was so fearful of losing what he had gained that he simply lost it and immediately felt better.

War serves this purpose as well. As long as conflict and tension can be identified, man is "happy." But as soon as they become covert or internalized, an enemy must be created.

Externalization is one of the best tactics a Toxick Magician can employ once he knows how to build internal tension in others without causing a rebound effect.

Build tension in others and help them find a scapegoat. Do this in small and insignificant ways until you have the power and ability to move people to more gross and hideous behaviors.

Help people realize how easy it is to lose the things they have or want. The trick in all of this is to not become identified as the bearer of bad tidings—unless you are looking for people with a strong stomach.

To learn better how to help people achieve the level of tension and conflict they can tolerate, begin by learning how to assess other people's moods. Once you are expert in this, learn how to manipulate their moods in simple ways.

Once you have this tactic mastered so that it is second nature, learn to assess moods and say things from time to time which will have significant effect.

Learn to say things to people *indirectly*. A useful way to do this is to communicate your message by talking to someone other than your victim.

For example, if you want to tell someone that they are an idiot, do not say so directly. Instead, make up a story about a fictitious person and tell it to another person in the same room as your victim.

This can also be done even more indirectly by telling the story to someone when the victim is not even present—if you know that the person to whom you tell the story will spread it in the direction you want it to go.

Learn to spread rumors in ways which will create concern, suspicion or trust. Create fires and then put them out. This technique is essential in building trust and confidence in people you want to use later.

Learn to confuse people and then help them out of their confusion. Remember, loyalty built on fear and hope is more reliable than loyalty built on friendship.

Friendships, no matter how good and how long they have lasted, are bound to turn on you at critical moments. Expect no one to take your punishment for you and expect no one *not* to take advantage of you if they can be assured that they will not be caught.

People have a tendency to change the rules of the game at a time that is convenient for them. Always keep this in mind and watch for the cues which will tell you that someone is about to change the rules.

If there is too much tension in a situation, be prepared for a rule change. If things seem too simple and easy, get ready for a "theft" of some sort. People like to get away with a little "stealing" from time to time. Give them the opportunity, as it will make them feel fragmented, weak and guilty and you can use this to your advantage.

These techniques will not work on a Toxick Magician. Do not make the mistake of miscalculating your opponents or your position on the food chain.

It is always unpleasant to find out that you are the one being eaten instead of the other way around. However, if this does happen, use it as a learning opportunity. It is rare that a person has the opportunity to learn from a real Master.

20

The Toxick Magician is forever alert to the fact that, to increase his accuracy in manipulating common people, he must continually scan the environment for appropriate reinforcers. He must know what will increase the chances of getting others to do what he wants.

Often a reinforcer can be as simple as a smile. At other times, however, a reinforcer can be quite complex, consisting of multiple categories of behaviors or items as well as multiple contingencies.

After much self-training, the Practitioner always asks himself questions about the environment and the humans operating in it. He is always aware of the limitations of a situation.

He is constantly examining the important social reinforcers within any given context. He determines the pecking order and notices which people are most easily influenced by approval or disapproval.

He is especially alert to anyone in authority with excellent social skills as he knows that such a person could also be a Toxick Magician.

He knows that a good Practitioner avoids direct confrontation and frequently speaks obliquely in order not to offend people or make them feel small. A person who is expert at this type of behavior can, at will, devastate someone by very simple means. Common people are easily hurt by someone who has been kind and friendly toward them and who they look up to.

The Practitioner knows how to use discomfort at just the right time to influence the effectiveness of a worker or an associate.

As a rule, a good Manipulator—or "Manager"—is secretly admired and envied by most of his subordinates. If the Manager is having problems with a subordinate, he immediately swings into action to correct the situation. He normally doesn't wait until unacceptable behavior gets worse. He uses office politics—or whatever else it might take—to change the behavior of the offender.

It is very important to realize that the Toxick Manager looks upon people as "cooperators" or "offenders." He doesn't take any behavior personally and is willing to do just about anything to correct damages and reduce the probabilities of negative outcomes.

A good Manipulator knows how to change the offender's behavior by having him perform tasks unrelated to the offensive behavior. Some minor privilege may be manipulated, although not taken away.

An event that the offender was looking forward to might be delayed by some "accident"—orchestrated by the Toxick Manager.

He is well aware that some people do not respond well to verbal communications and, thus, he requires a large bag of dirty tricks to correct the offensive behavior.

21

The Toxick Magician is always aware that, no matter how large a person may be, no matter how many degrees or years of experience he may have, common people are fundamentally children and must be treated as children without their becoming aware of the process.

One of the main themes of childhood is the gaining of information. This is called "learning" and adults do a fine job of making children stupid by their methods of indoctrination.

Compared to adults, children have minimal information. On the other hand, children have less perceptual and cognitive bias than adults.

For both the adult and the child, information is constantly being redefined, not only in content, but also in terms of how real information is defined. Put simply, real information consists of learning how to ignore and select data.

For example, forty years ago few children had much information about sex. Today, sex is so common that it is not really information at all. Once everything becomes available to everyone, it becomes nothing for everyone.

People appear more sophisticated today but, as the gross level of sophistication rises, the real information becomes more hidden and valuable.

When you hear an advertisement "disclose", "Be the first to know what the markets are doing," remember that it is being heard by millions of people at once. Where is the real information? It's mostly in the fact that millions of people each think they are hearing the real information first.

This is the illusion that TV provides: that you and those around you—alone—are being entertained. In fact, the more that people feel isolated yet tied together, the easier it is for the Master to reign.

He knows that real information "can't" be known. If real information could be had by everyone, it would immediately become worthless. Information, by its very definition, implies ignorance and exclusivity. We require ignorance in order to be informed. What most people *call* information is nothing more than another level of noise. Some optimists who are aware of the problem simply state that the information is available but the use of the information is still dependent on the intelligence of the population. Mass intelligence is nothing more than mass information. Zero is still zero.

What is fascinating about this entire process is that everyone thinks they know more but, in fact, they know less.

Moreover, what they *do* know is next to useless and is often *mis*-information. Thus, each new level of information is nothing more than a higher level of non-sense. What we generally call information is nothing more than a higher level of incompetence.

People forget that, like individuals, each civilization rises to its highest level of incompetence.

The Toxick Magician knows that if you help someone or something long enough, it will finally wish to be left alone. At that point help it a bit more and then drop it. At that point it will become like England: a land of non-entities with expensive titles.

This is the meaning of what we call information. The more teachers, the dumber the students.

Every mother's son simply knows more buzz words. But does that mean he knows what the buzzing is? Is it a bee or a bomb?

How much real wealth and how much real information does anyone *really* have? And, more importantly, how long will they have it? Wealth which can be easily stolen is not wealth at all. Most people are simply storehouses for a master thief.

With more and more reliance placed on devices which can be easily intercepted and manipulated, how long will it take for a Toxick collapse? These issues are important considerations for the Master.

His goal is to help information become more worthless while creating the illusion that it has more value. He does this by helping people ask more questions in very well-controlled and well-defined situations.

He also promotes the collapse by helping criminalize behavior which interferes with the information highway.

He knows that the criminalization of human behavior serves one primary purpose: the destruction of the system which defines crime. The more criminals, the more resources necessary to control crime and criminals. The more resources required, the more economic disruption and, thus, the more criminals required to fill the gaps in the system.

22

All mega-systems become top-heavy and chaotic. This is much like a family with more children than funds available to feed them. The parents become desperate to hold together the fortress that their egos had built.

The Toxick Magician knows that every structure serves to keep people *in* as well as *out*. As long as there are doors, there will be prisons.

The key is to get the prisoner to pay you for services that he could provide better for himself. Thus, the first task is to teach him that he can't care for himself and requires assistance. Once he accepts his dependency on metaphysical grounds and submits, his ownership is guaranteed.

Slavery, as we knew it before (for example) the Civil War in the U.S., was a bad thing. It made us aware of something best forgotten—universal, hierarchical slavery.

When overt slavery ended, we lost our example of what slavery was *really* all about. Slavery slipped back into our unconscious.

All good Practitioners know how to manipulate the common man's desire to be a slave while maintaining the illusion of being a free person. It is better for the common man to think that he is free as he is held in the arms of his caretaker.

Democracy is the best political system of slavery ever invented. In a democracy, the slaves believe that they are "free" and have a "voice" in their affairs. Thus, they are *willing* slaves and, as such, the possibility of a revolt is much less than in an overt system of slavery.

This simple fact is supported by the number of books which have been written about self-esteem. The desired results are impossible to obtain since a slave can only have false self-esteem. And even this is a theft accomplished by identifying with his master.

There are no free people—only slaves who have more privileges than others. Even the masters are slaves to their greed and terror. Control over the lives of millions doesn't free one from having to pay the price.

There are no real successes in this world as we are all bound in the brotherhood of death. If you have to die, you have failed.

23

One of the most important ideas to get through your head is that most people do not feel pain from being used—and misused—by a good Toxick Magician. If they feel any pain at all, it is minimal.

The fact of the matter is simple: people are so familiar with abuse and misuse that they are unaware of it. This is worth repeating. Most people are so used to being abused that for all intents and purposes they are unaware that they are being abused and, in most cases, expect it.

More interesting is the fact that, when they *do* feel abused, they get upset by events and actions which make them unaware of their real condition and the chronic abuse which they "suffer."

Moreover, they take the events of life, both good and bad, very personally. This fact alone contributes to their overall sense of malaise and stupidity. They are hard-wired to suffer and, in most cases, to suffer without much awareness. A deadened suffering is the norm and is expected.

Understanding the origin of human behavior is like looking for a place to land a plane when the earth below is covered by a huge, thick cloud. Human behavior makes no sense from a hedonic point of view, nor does it make sense from any alternative idea.

The human being is an unfinished entity, burdened by a strange mix of cortical and sub-cortical processes and a body which requires immense artifices to protect and assure it of its immortality.

24

One thing we know—very well—is that most humans have been hired on as extras. They are needed for this scene or that, for a few moments here and there, and then they are gone. In fact, they are not even forgotten—because to be forgotten you first have to be remembered.

Most people are extras who somehow have become deluded into thinking they are stars—albeit burnt-out ones.

A few people are not extras on the stage but are stunt men, hired to play dangerous roles for the real star. But even stunt men are rare.

· It's funny to walk into a bank or a grocery store and watch the tellers and clerks. A good Toxick Magician knows how to watch them and manipulate them. He knows that they feel that they have a little power—and they do—but they are taught not to abuse it, because it is a sign of bad taste.

Just watch them drool as they count out the money or say "no" to someone. Then watch them hang their little heads as they gaze blankly at their paychecks.

Nonetheless, each is a star, each has a room somewhere where he is king. Somewhere people recognize them as they perform their daily chores. Watch the smiles on their faces when you recognize them. Watch how some try to hold back their enthusiasm—like a dead puppy dog.

Others flaunt their authority like a bit player who has 30 seconds on second camera. But the Practitioner knows who these people really are. He, and even they, are not completely fooled.

They are the extras, the hired hands. They perform a service which some ape or machine could do as well—and someday, very soon, will. They are completely expendable, and those higher up the ladder know all too well how their middle management part can quickly revert to head clerk.

A Toxick Magician will treat such people as important or unimportant depending on his mood and what he wants from them.

Oh yes, Toxick Magicians have moods, too. And yes, they like to see the extras twitch once in a while. After all, life is tough, and watching someone squirm a bit can sometimes be uplifting— particularly if they are interfering with your will.

However, more often than not, it pays to be "nice" to the hired help. The Manipulator is well aware that the clerk can become a monster once someone in authority allows him to play a short part as boss. There is nothing more funny than seeing the little man inflate his chest and try to walk in shoes that are too long and not wide enough.

After his first day on the new job everyone feels sorry for him. Somehow he doesn't fit the part.

But soon enough no one will notice the difference. Many of the extras will have gone, some of the audience will have moved on, and the star—well, who can tell? Is her new billing for real, or is it just another temp job, waiting until someone better comes along?

In a strange way it takes a lot of strength or a powerful numbing agent to realize how insignificant you really are, what minor roles you play, and how everything you "love" and cherish can be taken away from you in the wink of a gnat's eye.

But this is the simple truth, and most people are constantly made unaware of their real situation. This keeps them tame and prevents them from revolt.

25

Every Toxick Magician finds out exactly what things a person is frightened to lose. And one of the most obvious and primal is their apparent sense of freedom.

That this feeling consists of nothing but the "freedom" to choose more or less what to eat, to come and go as they please (more or less), to say what's on their mind (more or less), to buy what they want, to stay up late, to have sex, to try something illicit once in a while, to spend money on things they like, is a joke. Is this all there is?

As a grown-up he is acutely aware (and yet, *must* keep secret from himself) that all these privileges which have been given to him, these "rights" which he has "earned"—can, all at once, for no good reason, be taken away.

Why must this be kept secret?

Because he has been told that he can lose them only if he *deserves to*—that is, if he does something wrong, if he disobeys. The Practitioner is completely aware of this horrifying lie and often needs to go no further in planning his strategies.

He knows what everyone is frightened of and why they are frightened. He knows that people believe that they have been *given* rights and privileges and, from their personal experience, they are completely correct. Of course, in reality no one has given anyone anything.

The Master has it one up on everyone: he knows that he really doesn't own anything. He knows that everything is borrowed—including his life.

Common man, however, always believes that which never was a reality. This ability comes from a strong imagination and the inability to distinguish the existential condition of his life from his hopes, wishes and dreams. In this sense, common man lives in limbo. He can neither climb the mountain, nor descend to hell.

26

If, from time to time, the Toxick Magician sounds like someone who concocted Huxley's Brave New World, let me assure you he is not. Indeed, as a matter of perversity, we might assume that Huxley was himself a Master with a keen knack for observing human behavior and who projected forward from what he saw.

While common man is competitive, greedy and ambitious—unlike Huxley's common worker-bee—this is only a small anomaly. Common man, as so many brilliant and stupid authors have noted, is simply a domesticated primate. And the zoo runs quite well, most of the time, until any of the many zero hours is reached—at which time pandemonium breaks loose.

While common man is domesticated, seething within him are all the necessary components of destruction which allow him to be controlled and, at the same time, allow him to be self-destructive. In this way, common man has the potential to act as if he were a sower of discord and disobedience, but this remains well under control—except during certain times of the year and in certain places.

Other than pathological individuals (including Toxick Magicians who have lost control), common man is nicely controlled by bouts of depression, temper tantrums, guilt, sorrow, terror and fear. The result of all of these emotions: common man is nullified—which allows for his ability to perform the rather pathetic and puny tasks to which he and others have given significance.

Manual II

Toxick Calculus: The Process of De-Education

by
Christopher S. Hyatt, Ph.D.

and
Dr. Jack S. Willis

The strength of a man is a function of his beliefs. The more he has, the weaker he is.
— Christopher S. Hyatt, Ph.D.

In the depths of my heart, I can't help being convinced that my fellowmen, with a few exceptions, are worthless.
— Sigmund Freud

Justice is no excuse for law.
— Iraqi Bar Association

I am against power until I have more than you.
— The wife of Dr. X

There are very few men who expend their life for themselves and unintentionally benefit us all. These are the most evil men of all.
— CSH

To Take Joy In Yourself Is The Greatest Crime.
— CSH

Definitions

Toxic(k): Capable of brain change, power, becoming who you are, especially byntiveness, practice, will, deceit, and study.

Calculus: a. The branch of mathematics that deals with limits and the differentiation and integration of functions of one or more variables. b. A method of analysis or calculation using a special symbolic notation. c. The combined mathematics of differential calculus and integral calculus.

Toxick Calculus: The mathematics of power.

Two Notes to Get the Time-Wasters and the Academics Out of the Way

A. I have written this book in the way I wanted to write it......not for the ease of the reader nor for the sake of favorable reviews.

There are enough self-help books which are based on sitcoms. (This means I am not here to make you feel good.) And, as far as reviews go, I prefer to buy them.

B. I am not here to argue with the reader......this I leave to the sophomore. I am here to search for truth—as unpleasant and elegant as it may turn out to be. I am here to help you explore yourself and, by doing this, provide myself with more power.

The Code of Psychopathic Conduct—CPC

CPC122.6: The two statements above are direct and confrontative. Statements of this kind should be avoided unless you are fairly certain of the results. They are a luxury of power and should normally be confined to your sphere of influence.

CPC132.9: The President does not tell the average person that he is the President. Nor does he normally tell his enemies. He simply acts with just enough power......also he never wounds a real enemy. He destroys them, using more power than necessary. He then shows mercy to some of his enemies' subordinates.

CPC843.0X: Even fools have their uses.

THE MAJORITY OF MEN HAVE BEEN DEALT CARDS TO A GAME THEY DO NOT KNOW HOW TO PLAY

The Problem

Man is born in bondage.
We must ask, bondage to what?
The answer? To his own nature.

How can man overcome his bondage?
By mastering himself.

How has this been attempted?

Through the following methods:

FEAR

Fear of punishment.
Fear of Government.
Fear of each other.
Fear of nature.
Fear of Self.
Fear of God.

FEAR

What has been accomplished?
The Beast in the Mirror.

The Goal

"What is good? — All that heightens the feeling of power,
the will to power, power itself in man.

What is bad? — all that proceeds from weakness.

What is happiness? — The feeling that power increases —
that a resistance is overcome.

Not contentment, but more power; not peace at all, but war; not virtue, but proficiency (virtue in the Renaissance style, virtu, virtue free of moralic acid).

The weak and ill-constituted shall perish: first principle of our philanthropy.

And one shall help them to do so.

What is more harmful than any vice? — Active sympathy for the ill-constituted and weak — Christianity...

The problem I raise here is not what ought to succeed mankind in the sequence of species (—the human being is an end—): **but what type of human being one ought to breed, ought to will, as more valuable, more worthy of life, more certain of the future.**

This more valuable type has existed often enough already: but as a lucky accident, as an exception, never as willed. He has rather been the most feared, he has hitherto been virtually the thing to be feared — and out of fear the reverse type has been willed, bred, achieved: the domestic animal, the herd animal, the sick animal man—the Christian..."

— F.W. Nietzsche, *The Anti-Christ*

CPC176.a9: Keep in mind that 90% of all humans are nothing more than talking, breeding monkeys in costume. They are constantly being tossed between greed and fear.

Rules to keep in mind:

a. You will find a person greedy, or satisfied for the moment; you will find a person fearful, or secure for the moment. If both fear and greed are satisfied, you will find a person bored/seeking or depressed...... If either/or both fear and greed are active you will find a person motivated... If over-active you will find the person manic and/or depressed... Learn to identify these states from observation...and then learn how to manipulate one state into the other......

> b. Do not pay attention to what they *say*; attend only to what they have *done* and what they are *doing*. If you find yourself getting lost in their ideals, titles, and possessions, simply imagine them in diapers sucking on a bottle, or lying quietly in their grave. Always keep in mind that humans are animals. Think of everyone as a five-year-old.
>
> c. Finally, never be fooled by their education or their talents...... They don't know how to apply their learning to themselves or others once removed from their roles & labels. Remember, they live and "think" through labels and are incapable of perceiving reality clearly. This means that you can get them to jump through hoops by simply manipulating their labels...... If you find them doing something which interferes with your plans, simply "throw" them a tasty label and watch them munch their way through it.

Design Errors & the World of Unruly Chance

The frontal lobes—the executive, rational thinking centers—are easily influenced by the lower brain, while the lower brain is not easily influenced by the executive, thinking centers. This alone has such overwhelming implications that volumes could, and should, be written.

What we think and the thoughts we have are motivated—distorted by our innate nature, but not the other way around. The primary forces are fear, aggression and power. These traits are present in everyone......use them for your benefit. Reflect well!

We are inherently irrational, although we like to fancy ourselves as rational beings......the truth is simple: we are irrational beings capable of rational thought.

In addition, the protracted state of dependency and defenselessness of the human infant make it highly susceptible to imprinting and early learning which is increasingly difficult to erase as the organism matures. Thus, the errors and irrationality of the previous generation are easily passed forward. The belief that education can modify these early errors and innate tendencies are more a dream than an actuality. So-called "socialization"— which is innate for humans—simply disguises what is really there and makes it more difficult for us to redesign ourselves......

We are the only living creatures on earth that have the ability to re-design ourselves. However, this fact horrifies the monkey-man. Few humans can think clearly about their own lives and thus truly transform themselves into the higher type.

Another difficulty is that the lower brain centers not only talk to and influence the higher brain centers, but also talk within and between themselves. This means that, while some early conditioning can be modified, under intense stress the lower centers activate previous learning within and between the lower brain centers.

Another design problem is that we are fundamentally social animals. The parts of the brain in which memories are stored are at various distances from the part of the brain associated with emotional activity: closest are the memories related to human relationships; next closest are the memories related to animals; and next are the memories associated with tools. This means that our highly dependent periods of imprinting act as if they are more or less hard-wired. Research on the brains of stroke patients show that the memory centers associated with lower social brain activity are *physically* closer to the emotional brain than memories associated with tools. This has vast and broad implications. Write one concise paragraph about what these implications might be.

Was Aristotle the First Psychopath?

"A person is thought to be great-souled if he claims much and deserves much... He that claims less than he deserves is small-souled... The truly great-souled man must be a good man...

Greatness of soul seems...a crowning ornament of all the virtues... Great honours accorded by persons of worth will afford *[the great-souled man]* pleasure in a moderate degree: he will feel he is receiving only what belongs to him, or even less, for no honour can be adequate to the merits of perfect virtue, yet all the same he will deign to accept their honours, because they have no greater tribute to offer him.

Honour rendered by common people and on trivial grounds he will utterly despise, for this is not what he merits... He therefore to whom even honour is a small thing will be indifferent to other things as well. Hence great-souled men are thought to be haughty...

The great-souled man is justified in despising other people—his estimates are correct; but most proud men have no good ground for their pride... He is fond of conferring benefits, but ashamed to receive them, because the former is a mark of superiority and the latter of inferiority.

He returns a service done to him with interest, since this will put the original benefactor into his debt in turn, and make him the party benefited. The great-souled are said to have a good memory for any benefit they have conferred, but a bad memory for those which they have received (since the recipient of a benefit is the inferior of his benefactor, whereas they desire to be superior)...

It is also characteristic of the great-souled men never to ask help from others, or only with reluctance, but to render aid willingly; and to be haughty towards men of position and fortune, but courteous towards those of moderate station...and to adopt a high manner with the former is not ill-bred, but it is vulgar to lord it over humble people... He must be open both in love and in hate, since concealment shows timidity; and care more for the truth than for what people will think; ...he is outspoken and frank, except when speaking with ironical self-deprecation, as he does to common people. He will be incapable of living at the will of another, **unless a friend**, since to do so is slavish... He does not bear a grudge, for it is not a mark of greatness of soul to recall things against people, especially the wrongs they have done you, but rather to overlook them. He is...not given to speaking evil himself, even of his enemies, except when he deliberately intends to give offence... Such then being the great-souled man, the corresponding character on the side of deficiency is the small-souled man, and on that of excess the vain man."

— Aristotle

And what might a vain man be? Someone who deserves little and demands a lot.

CPC356.0: "It is smarter to give than to receive." However, giving too much will create hostility in the recipient. It often becomes a debt which the person can't pay back—except by harming you. But learn how to use this: give too much and, if you are punished, use it to your benefit......guilt is its own reward.

CPC689.we: Although it is important to express strong feeling from time to time, doing so too often will make you seem weak in the eyes of others. Not being able to control the expression of your emotions will cost you dearly. Time your temper tantrums—throw one when least expected, then ask to be forgiven...... Most often, you won't.

CPC974.0: When it is time to punish someone, decide whether or not an audience should be present. Humiliating someone in public can make a docile dog more docile, but a vain and bitter dog revengeful. Be sure to understand the nature of your victim. Learn to be an expert in using the "nature survey" provided below.

CPC863.o: Treat an inferior fairly; however, do not let him know that you know how he really feels about himself. Keep in mind that most people feel inferior. This is evidenced both by those who frequently act out and by those who appear very humble. The humble type is bitter and more dangerous. Remember, the humble person prides himself on his humility. When a person is being especially humble, be silly...... If he looks hurt......tell him you are sorry......and say that your laughter was not directed toward him... This will make him distrust you and make mistakes.

CPC009.7: Let weaker people help you in insignificant matters. Be sure to show a little more gratitude than the person deserves.

CPC231.99a: As most people are sheep, kind words are both cheap and effective. Use them at the right time but also randomly......use them when the person is behaving badly... I once transformed a professor by telling him his hostile behavior was simply the only way he knew how to tell people he really cared... He agreed. I was the only person to understand him. He was in my debt.

CPC052.76: Treat a man who is full of himself with occasional random praise. Never praise him for what he does well, but only for what he does poorly.

CPC874.81: Treat petty people with power with kindness and respect......but be cautious of over-indulging them... They are acutely aware of how dependent they are on their titles and their superiors. When a policeman gives you a ticket, tell him you are going to write a letter to his superiors telling them how he turned an unpleasant experience into a humane encounter. Get a pen out and write down his badge number, the time and place of the ticket, etc.... You will scare and confuse him... Be gracious......

A Three Minute Peep Show
A Little Poison Anyone—?
Taking the Cure May Kill You

The nature of the mind *is* to create both meaning and an interdependency of all ideas. The cure is the realization that life is a whole and that division—as created by mind and language—are man's attempt to overcome himself. In other words, man is a powerful and creative joyous fool. In his attempts to overcome himself, he has caused himself to forget his creativeness and power. How does this work?

In the reality of the moment man is naked. He looks for power over himself and his environment. His power of creativity is so great that he creates ideas and *acts as if they have an independent existence.* He believes them to be true—independent of his will to create them. When the mortar hardens he is trapped—having forgotten that he has made the concrete.

> *Now, this is man's greatest power: the ability to forget your power. God did it!*

Man is particularly creative in the areas of metaphysics. He creates beginnings, endings, values, purposes, morals, causes, time, justice, things-in-themselves, laws, order, right, wrong; and then he *forgets* that they are *his inventions.* If he remembered that he invented them, his pain would be overwhelming. He would "live" in nihilism or he would become our hero: the psychopath.

CPC3593.5: The human brain is hungry for causality. This is a primitive survival mechanism which, through great suffering and struggle, mankind has refined into the scientific method. However, most humans never bother applying this most hard-won accomplishment to their daily lives. Your job is to provide people with the causalities which best suit your purposes. Lacking explanations for both good and bad events, humans invent "causes." Inventing "reasons" like god, spirits, and a morass of other nonsense fill the void that fear and the inability to think have created. Creating causes which involve intrigue, enemies, bias, etc. are particularly interesting for these infantile creatures. When events occur which have no obvious cause, help people find "answers" which suit you. This method is particularly good in the workplace and in social gatherings. If you are good at this, you will increase your personal and social wealth.

Man's creations become "necessities" that stifle and limit him. No longer is he living in the moment, having projected and given his power away; he begs and prays to be free again. What he can't tolerate is the idea that there is *no one* to give him his freedom. It is right where he sits—now—but this freedom is a great horror.

EXERCISE 4.6

Look at your belief/meaning system......and attempt to rid yourself of it for a day...... Watch and record what happens......

An example of a cure: Pity

The cure is to show you how your pity for others is simply a device to cover up your own vulnerability. Your sighs and groans of concern are simply for yourself. You support weakness because you are too weak to stand the blade of the knife as it passes through your illusions. And what is this illusion? That your desire to overcome yourself—the desire for power over yourself and life —has now enslaved you. And how do you maintain your illusions? Forgetfulness. Ask yourself how many people do you "keep" around you to support your enslavement? This is one purpose of the family.

The Altruist

You have convinced yourself that you are nothing and wish everyone else to be nothing. You are vain and weak and hide behind your concern for mankind. Do not feel guilty for your wealth and accomplishments; don't apologize by pretending to yourself that it is for the benefit of others.

The Lover of Man

If you really love man and wish to help him—stick him with a pitchfork. Stick him hard enough so he can hear his own screams —stick him hard and if he hears himself cry and drops the illusion, it does not matter what else happens—it can only be in the service of him. There is no more time to string the beast along. Stick him or leave him alone. Show him how creative and powerful he has been in creating his heavens and hells.

> CPC4325.9: Avoid helping people improve themselves unless you value them or want them indebted to you. Keep in mind that most people will not improve themselves no matter what you do... In fact, you can destroy them if you help them too much... Be kind from time to time......

The Egoist

The brain that creates beauty also creates tragedy. The brain that solves the riddle of the cosmos and the mathematics of quantum electrodynamics also creates the myths that destroy, weaken, enslave, ensnare and paralyze. The psychopath acknowledges that he is born a fool and is living in an insane asylum. He does not seek to make sense of the senseless, he does not look to find reason in chaos. Being convinced that those about him are nuts, he commits to the law of the self rather than the blatherings of the herd.

You know about those "huddled masses yearning to be free"? Well, the psychopath refuses to be huddled, he refuses to be one of the masses, he refuses to yearn. The psychopath does not yearn—he *does*, he *is*. The psychopath says violence and compulsion are in the slave and his master—freedom is in me. I choose freedom and I will live it. The psychopath does not advertise his specialness—he knows that the masses must destroy the different. He prospers in secret away from the envious eyes of the herd.

> CPC86.av: Learn what concerns the sheep and offer them assistance; and always let them know that they deserve the handout. Be sure to turn every weakness into a virtue, every failure into a success. Never forget that *reality is that last thing people want to know about.*

BUY A JOURNAL

Read the quote (below) very slowly. In your journal write down your first reactions. Wait three minutes and then read it very fast. Whatever your reactions were, contradict them, tell yourself the exact opposite of what you wrote down.

Think of all the people you pity—write down their names on a piece of paper—and then burn it......of course, include your own name... Yell, "No pity."

Stop here, go back and reread everything which you have just read and count the number of spelling errors...... Write the number down in your journal.

"This more valuable type has existed often enough already: but as a lucky accident, as an exception, never as willed. He has rather been the most feared, he has hitherto been virtually the thing to be feared — and out of fear the reverse type has been willed, bred, achieved: the domestic animal, the herd animal, the sick animal man — the Christian..."
— F.W. Nietzsche, *The Anti-Christ*

Conclusions A1

So we now have come to the definition of **OUR GOAL**: to create, to will, to provide a *culture* where this lucky bacteria might grow......however we also must de-educate; undo; remove beliefs, conditioned reflexes, irrational fears......and, at the same time, grow new brain tissue. A worthy task?

The Psychopath is Not the Sociopath

Dictionary definitions notwithstanding, there is a simple difference between the psychopath and the sociopath: the sociopath is against people and himself. He is dependent, he needs to harm others to be himself.

The psychopath exists for himself......other people are simply there—as allies, obstacles, tools—but mostly they are just there......he causes no harm for harm's sake......he stands for more life, joy, power, and freedom for himself and his own kind.

You've heard about people who are co-dependent? How about people who are co-*independent*. The psychopath needs others for their *values*, not for their weaknesses. The psychopath lives, others exist. To steal from Thoreau, the mass of men leads lives as corks on the ocean of life; the psychopath *is* the ocean. The psychopath does not look to others to create his happiness; he creates his own.

CPC003.87: The psychopath accepts that survival and struggle are the basics of existence... With style, he works to his end, at all times increasing the quality of his existence.

Is This Zehm Alohim?

EXERCISE 16.9

Develop an entire separate life in an area away from your hunting grounds. Become someone else, make up a story, create new friends and associates. Make yourself into a mystery...... Try out your new talents in this setting, if you fail, move on to another locale and start up again...... I have two or three areas where I practice different styles on people. I have completely different names and stories. In one location I am a successful businessman; in another, I am a bum whose wife and children left him.

We Are Elitists

We are Elitists and we desire to assist others in their quest for elitism.

We have no use for the weak and the lame. The starving children and their parents are simply food.

From our point of view, altruism is a disease: the psychology of death.

We don't value the welfare morality or the death cries of trash.

We do not want approval, except from those *we value*. Hopefully, for some of you, this will be offensive; for others it will be a breath of fresh mountain air. If this is true, we have accomplished our goal. With this said we will move on.

You are a Criminal
Accept It
Stop Fighting

In the world today, everyone is a criminal. The only issue for "the authorities" is: are you worth *bothering with now*?

Anyone who has drawn a breath has broken a law.

No matter what your position or title, you can be broken when it suits those who have absolute immunity to employ violence, kidnapping, torture and confiscation.

For most people, finding truth is not what it is all about. What is important is the appearance of order—known by lawyers as "due process"......

Due process simply means going through the prescribed motions to soothe the terror of the sheep. However, the results are the same as the threat of a firing squad: obey or else. (In passing, when I was taking a post-doctoral course in criminal justice, we were asked to write a lengthy paper comparing various laws by cultures, countries, states, etc. We were asked to find what was common amongst them. Some students wrote "laws against murder," etc. I simply wrote: "OBEY." *This* is the common fundamental factor of all laws: "OBEY...or else!")

A number of sociologists have disagreed with me. They have said that laws against murder and rape are fundamental and necessary. (Oh, really? Every feudal society has at least one class which can commit murder and rape with impunity—as long as it is done outside their class.) Regardless of their factual inaccuracy, however, they have missed the point. "What is the purpose of law," I ask? Usually they give lengthy answers involving issues such as "social order." They do not seem to understand that, underlying all law (whether the Torah with its 613 laws, or US Federal law; and regardless of what the law is) its "metastructure" is *Obey the Law*. If you don't obey the law there are consequences which, of course, are backed by the threat of violence. It does not matter *what* is obeyed, as much as that *you must obey*——from cradle to grave. Thus, the sociologist must recognize that whatever comprises the social fabric, its fundamental nature is obedience to whomever is in charge.

CPCa231.9: The psychopath must be able to act as if he is socialized while, at the same time, quietly observing and acting from a position of social indifference. He must act involved in the petty concerns of those around him while standing back, pulling the strings. Who said, "I stood among them but was not of them"?

EXERCISE 26.3

Go to a church this Sunday; get yourself invited to an after-church social event... watch them with a smile on your face and the cold dead eyes of the shark...... This is it! this is —what it— is all about......

CPCn924.9: People believe that they have rights... They are idiots. Rights last only as long as the ammunition...... The psychopath reminds people of their rights, all the time knowing that everyone is a moment away from complete slavery. The best method to enslave people is to tell them that they are free. Help them believe that every necessity was a choice......

CPC0-9.e: Get people to help other people. It makes them feel good and they will never forget who they helped. Create random chaos......through good deeds. Buy extra copies of this book and leave them in churches, toilets and police stations.

Terror Alert

A message from the other side from Dr. Regardie:
"Remember, children: We are all monkeys here! ¡Hee Hee Hee!"

Interlude

Listen to the news for one hour every day for a month......but listen as you have never listened before. Make a recording of at least two different news channels; compare and contrast their styles, define their basic assumptions about human nature, and their assumptions about what the audience believes. Define their style of manipulation...pay close attention to who pays for their time.

Dupe Alert

There are three ways to lie: by deliberate mis-statement; by leaving out relevant facts; by adding irrelevant facts. News programs use all three methods.

The *New York Times* often lies by mist-statement. One famous example was their defense of Fidel Castro as an "agrarian reformer" when it was well known that he was a communist.

Lying by leaving out relevant facts is shown in the reporting of the shootings at Columbine High School. Almost no one pointed out that teachers were forbidden to have guns and, therefore, the students had lots of time to kill the maximum number of people because everyone at the school was defenseless. The number of people killed was a result of gun control which prevented any self-defense.

Lying by adding irrelevant "facts" is shown by the talk of the looting at the Baghdad Museum. Most public artifacts had been moved out of the museum before the war started and the greatest number of missing exhibits were from the locked vaults for which keys were only in the possession of the museum executives. But the news programs report that thousand of exhibits were missing and showed pictures of smashed vases.

Without being a news-junky, you can't be expected to know all the lies; but you can listen to all news with the assumption in mind that at all times you are being lied to, manipulated, and treated like a member of the unwashed (m)asses. Do not become hypnotised by what goes on around you. Remember: the world is simply masses of asses.

CPCh1212.09: *There is no such thing as hypnosis...* Keep in mind that the goal of this book is to *de-hypnotize.* To this end you should read Steven Heller's *Monsters and Magical Sticks,* New Falcon Publications, 2001) ......most people are in a trance most of the time...except we call it conscious-ness... In fact, they are very much asleep.

Learn to manipulate people's sleep patterns by manipulat-ing their labels and beliefs... Remember, it is very easy to redefine where the sleepwalker is going...... Tell him that he is going to save the world from (?) and he will commit suicide...... If you call it suicide he will not do it, but if you call it "fighting for god," he will. People are not rational. Learn hypnosis, both the passive and the active forms of induction, and use it everyday on someone you meet. Keep in mind that all beliefs are nothing but conceptual hypnotic trances.

CPCxxx.00: Passing secret: you can easily make people do what they do not want to do—simply redefine it. Call mur-der "freedom"; call suicide "heroism"; call theft "helping the poor"; call imprisoning great men "justice"; tell the sleep-walker on the ledge that he can fly. –LOL–

CPC-0-0.0: Think of the herd as a poorly wired octopus. Absurdity is the norm. Break something at the next party you are invited to. Send an apology three weeks later.

Double Dupe Alert

Any statement by any government or group of govern(tor)mentors should be assumed to be a total lie.

When the federal looters pass a budget that increases spending by 500 billion dollars and then pass spending bills that only allocate 300 billion dollars, they call it a 200 billion dollar spending cut. When the looters increase spending but don't steal more in taxes, they call it a deficit because there are not enough taxes. The best one-liner on politicians I have ever heard is: *Have you ever seen someone get into office and turn honest?*

In the first two years of the George W. Bush administration, federal looters increased spending by 16% and blame the deficit on the "new" tax cut......which had not yet taken place.

EXERCISE 6.5

Watch three sitcoms for a month...... Now! you know what people value and what they compare themselves to...... Count their lies, their assumptions, their social tricks, how they inculcate values and ideals in the viewer. Record a few different sitcoms and begin to break them down. Notice how they use laughter to get the audience to accept their implicit values.

CPC631.LL: Don't answer stupidity with Rationality. You will lose. Answer stupidity with false praise......

Terror Alert

Belief: The Sign of a Crippled Mind

EVERY FOOL
THINKS HE HAS
SOMETHING
TO LOSE

Every person has a "right" to his beliefs, feelings and opinions...and every person has a right to be stupid. For most people, it is more important to assert their "independent" identity than to be correct, effective and powerful. This should tell us a lot: *Everyone has a right to be stupid*—and the more stupid they are, the better for you. Keep in mind that belief occurs when there are few—or no—facts... If you have lots of facts, then belief is absurd... Also remember that opinions belong to those who are experts and have few facts...... Help idiots believe that they are experts.

In the real world, with real people, there are a number of possible answers to any question; but before we get to those answers, we ask, *is the question really a question*?

Never assume that simply because some words are strung together to give the appearance of a question that it *is* a question. For example, "Does god exist?" Although this looks like a question it isn't. Why?

Could we set up an experiment to demonstrate that god exists? If you can't devise an experiment to demonstrate that something exists, the entire issue becomes absurd.

By the very definition of god, its existence can't be proven... God must be *believed in* and, as such, the so-called question is absurd. Another interesting point: the phrase "does god exist?" can only be looked at mythologically (i.e., pre-history); or religiously (i.e., belief with historical events—assumed calendar time); or philosophically (i.e., real calendar time) and requires "proof"—that is, it must be answered yes or no, but the answers are often flawed and incorrect. Why? Because arguments based on the mythical, religious and philosophical levels are loaded with a pyramid of hidden assumptions. Another problem is that often these "proofs" are simply analogies: e.g., if there is a watch, there has to be a watchmaker. The watch exists so, therefore, someone had to make it. But argument by analogy is no argument at all. All attempts to prove that god exists by reason, logic, and deduction are false—they involve massive logical errors.

All of this leads us to the world of the psychopath and the hard-won world of science (i.e., actuality); if it can't be answered empirically, it isn't a legitimate question at the present time. The psychopath is an empiricist. He lives in the world of actuality and not the world of metaphysics.

Credo quia absurdum [I believe because it is absurd]
— Tertullian

Was it really he who said this or...??? Write us.

Danger:
Thinking Causes Brain Growth

Proofs come in different flavors. Other than chocolate, vanilla, and strawberry there are existence proofs, causality proofs, statistical proofs, and best-fit proofs.

Memorize these—
Evolution uses a best-fit proof.
Psychology uses a statistical proof.
Astronomy uses a causality proof.
God requires an existence proof.

EXERCISE 46.6

Devise an experiment to show that unicorns exist.

Do the same for fire-breathing dragons, witches, and angels.

NOTE: **if you have a "Holy Guardian Angel," you may now close this book and throw it away. You are not suited to psychopathdom. If you need someone to protect you, hire a bodyguard—or buy a gun and learn to protect yourself. If you need to thank someone for your good fortune, send Dr. Hyatt his 10% tithe. If you need an explanation for your misfortune, break a mirror so you have a good excuse for at least seven more years.**

So, if a question *is* a question, we can attempt to find an answer and, broadly speaking, the answers can fall into a number of categories: yes, no, maybe, sometimes, don't know at this time. But life isn't as simple as that. A question that can be answered requires specific definitions for each term. Thus, it must specify who, what, where, how, and when before any meaningful answer can be given. For example the question, "Did Dr. Hyatt write this sentence?" is a real question; we have a who and a what...and we can specify where and how and we can define what proof would be needed to demonstrate that it was Dr. Hyatt who wrote this sentence. So the question is legitimate and we can investigate and find an answer: yes, no, can't be determined, maybe, I don't know.

EXERCISE 8.3

Prove that Dr. Hyatt is a figment of your wild imagination, also known as a nightmare. Hint: use any holy book from the *Egyptian Book of the Dead* to the *Book of Mormon*. You will never find him mentioned and thus you have a revealed source of knowledge that proves Dr. Hyatt is a malicious invention of a reincarnated heretic.

Secret note from Dr. Jack: Dr. Hyatt does have three eyes, horns, and a tail. His skin is pink pastel with chartreuse polka dots.

EXERCISE IMPERATIVE

List your friends, family and associates. Write down their fundamental beliefs; if you don't know what they are, find out. How *strong* are their beliefs? Use a scale from 1–10. Next, how might you change their beliefs without their knowing? Predict their verbal behavior when challenged about their beliefs and then compare their verbal behavior to their actions... Oh, and don't forget to include yourself.

CDC01313.y: The Trilogy of Defeat—

Most human beings have a secret "entitlement program." Deep down they believe that they are owed. The owing can take any form, so be alert. Learn to reinforce their feeling of entitlement. This makes people weaker by occupying them with the injustices that they have endured. It also helps them to remain passive, like an infant waiting for the breast. While they wait, you act.........

Find your own entitlement program...

Right along with the entitlement program is the "precious program." This program states that, no matter who and what I am, no matter how much I claim I hate myself, my personality is unique and "precious." Help people believe that they are even more precious then they believe they are. This will keep them waiting for the mystery reward from heaven, and prevent them from changing their way of life.

The precious personality program guarantees failure. To change, the pain of disintegration is required. As long as they perceive that their attitudes, habits and halo are precious, the necessary painful experiences required for change can't be effective.

Find your precious personality program.

Finally, not only do people feel entitled and precious, they believe that they are individuals—and many will have to show you how individual they are. Some will reject doing something your way even if doing so would yield a large potential profit. Instead they will do it their way to show you what an individual they are—even if it means failure. We have often enjoyed helping people do it their way......

Need we say more?

Solution to Being Stupid

Keep in mind that most people behave as if *stupidity is a virtue*. How many virtuous people have *you* met today?

Determine every belief you have and design a way to test it. If you can't test it, destroy it......

> TRUISM: In this world, ultimate flexibility and adaptability are essential. However, every adaptation must be an adjustment to the moment—it shouldn't exist in granite. When the moment is gone, the adjustment is gone. **The moral idealist will always lose to the man of passion, commitment and goal: the psychopath. A man who loves his work is a rare man indeed and he will always triumph over the moralist—the man who does his work for the "right" reason.**
>
> **What does this mean? Write it in your journal.**

The Secret

> CPC7567.w: Be capable of anything, at anytime, anywhere. Your first investment is yourself. Be the bank, banker and the depositor. Examine your books before you go to sleep each night and, while sleeping, devise plans for increasing your net worth. Help others make deposits in your bank. You can help them to do this by getting them to believe that they are helping themselves by helping you. Learn to give meaning to other people's lives...let them help a little.
>
> CPC1.h8: You must learn everything you can, believe everything others believe, and then believe nothing. **You become the chameleon while everyone else is becoming some—thing.** The psychopath is committed to himself and to what is necessary to expand himself and his life.
>
> CPC076.a From time to time throw money in the street. Or—use a public toilet and then place a $10 bill on top......and don't flush! Create random conflict by doing good deeds.

EXERCISE 9.5

Find someone you really admire—and I mean *really admire*. Watch him carefully and, after you feel you have an understanding of him, begin to imitate his manners, behavior, voice, gestures, etc.... Keep in mind that, if you are successful at this exercise, you will feel anxiety......your core personality will be threatened......this is a sign that your precious conditioned self is dissolving.

Now find someone you loathe and begin to imitate him. This will make you sick—another sign that you are dissolving.

Now become an orthodox (?). Become a True Believer, become a cheer leader for the cause. This may make you feel like you are dying—another sign you are dissolving.

Make love to a person you despise.

Ignore your extended family for three months...be distant, withdrawn, strange...... (If you have already been ignoring them, draw them close...) Then tell them that they have been correct and you have been wrong...... Ask for help... Take what they give you and blow it on things they despise......

Have you dissolved yet?

The Psychopath's Math

Mathematicians refer to something they call "a zero-sum game." That is, every winner implies a loser. Like poker.

Psychopaths have a "one-sum game." That is, I win and you can either win or lose depending on your own psychopath quotient. It is nice if we both win, but my job is to see that I win and your job is to see that you win. Psychopaths cooperate easily because they don't have an interest in the other person's losing. Non-psychopaths want either the other person to win (at their own altruistic expense), or they want both to win (and thus usually both lose), or they want to win while the other person loses. *Homo normalis* dies waiting for his turn to come. *Homo psychopathis* doesn't wait—he lives life to his fullest advantage all along.

The goal of life is living. If you think the goal of life is to get to the afterlife, then give this book to someone who deserves it.

If you think the goal of life is to impress someone with your possessions or looks or intelligence or...then you are not living— you are a circus act.

CPC357.7: If you are successful, buy toys which others approve of. Use symbols which instill respect in the minds of the weak. Wear cheap clothes from time to time, but make them look expensive......show others how much you need them to approve of you......but always do this in indirect ways. Appear to be working on something important......but are having a hard time. See if you can get someone to take an interest in your insane project......

CPC4141.k: If you have a lot of money, use it to support your secret projects...... When people ask you for money, tell them that it is tied up for your children's education...... Always give them a value that *they* value, not a value that *you* value...... Keep your real values to yourself and only share them with people worthy of them.

CPC970.p: Give people the opportunity to disappoint you from time to time—it instills guilt and guilt is debt.

CPC89: Allow others to hurt you, to take revenge in small things—this will put them in your debt.

CPC666: Learn to lose and reap rewards...... If you have a winning hand, lose once in a while...even if the pot is big.

CPCmn6: Learn to make small mistakes and let people help you correct your errors.

CPClq4: Keep in mind that most people are sado-masochists. Give them opportunities to act out. Help them degrade themselves in private and never bring it up to them...except once. They will expect it a second time, but never bring it up again......

Interlude Alert

Is This Zehm Alohim?

EXERCISE 2.16

For a few months, take a few hours every week and go to a church or temple...... Do not simply go to the services; go talk with the "Priest." Tell him that you have been an atheist all your life, but feel that something is missing in your life, that you have been unhappy and miserable, and you want to learn about God from his particular religious point of view.

Ask him to tell you how his religion is different from others and what can it offer you. Be polite, don't argue......just be stupid and ask simple questions. Ask how his particular religion will help you—ask about marriage, sex, children, work, donations. Ask him how he became involved with his particular sect...... Be sure to ask if belief in God is necessary. Remember, the Priest class is well-trained in seduction. He will measure you and try a number of test questions to determine what path to take......

Beliefs are like a soup line—lots of liquid, very little mass......

Belief: Something believed or accepted as true, especially a particular tenet or a body of tenets, simply because a person, an authority, or a number of persons assert it is true. Accepting a string of words as valid without any evidence. As Robert Anton Wilson says, "faith is stupidity" (Prometheus Rising, *New Falcon Publications, 1984*).

What passes for evidence is how much fear can be generated in the victim.

A person who believes *is a victim of fear, early learning, and ignorance. However, in most cases, stupidity can be substituted for ignorance.*

In fact, belief is a sure sign of a crippled mind. Things are either true or not true, or have a probability of truth. You can only know things that you can know now. You can't—by definition—know what can't be known now.

All assertions must answer the following questions: who, what where, how, and when...... Once these are answered with some degree of certainty, or determined that they can't be answered, then the content of the answer must be scrutinized.

Those Sacred Feelings

What we feel are "Automated Conclusions" (AC); they are largely determined by what we believe or assume to be true—that is "Automated 'thoughts'." Automated thoughts (AT) are not thinking. ACs, or Automated Conclusions are untested conclusions.

ACs are metaphysical in nature—that is, unstated assumptions which, by definition, can't be proven and hence can't be disproved...... This is their insidious nature. Thus, most people spend a good deal of their time either attempting to prove or disprove these ACs. But remember, these assumptions can't, by definition, be proved or disproved.

CPCah1: Let people be idiots. Let them believe that they are safe, have rights, have dignity... In fact, help them strengthen their beliefs... From time to time be sure to show them they are wrong, but don't tell them, just show them. Let them see evil be victorious......

CPCto98: **Remember: words are more real than reality.**

I will repeat this: words are more real than reality. Learn to manipulate words. Become a philologist, a lover of words...

EXERCISE 9.113

Buy three more copies of this book. Hand one to a stranger, one to a priest and one to a relative. (P.S. When ordering, ask for your psychopath's discount.)

Some of the Most Misused Words

What are some of the most misused words? Stop now! Don't continue reading! Determine the most misused word and then check it below.

STOP BEFORE LOOKING

Believe? Think? Want? Love? Must? Cannot? Feel?

Let us take, for example, the word "feel". People treat the word as though it were a magic potion that excuses all desires, whims, impulses, mistakes in thinking, irrationality, and ignorance. All you have to do is throw in "I feel" before any statement and then the statement is unchallengeable. "I feel defeated and so I *am* defeated and there is no possible course of action." "I feel you don't love me and that proves you don't love me." "I feel I can't live up to being a psychopath and therefore there is no reason to even start."

Most so-called feelings are not feelings at all—they are random thoughts, opinions, judgments, beliefs, prejudices—all of which reveal a lack of knowledge.

EXERCISE 12.4

Try to go one day without using, or even thinking, the words "I feel." Try to go two days. See how long you can go without saying or thinking those words. Even when you are tired at night, the right phrase is not "I feel tired"—it is "I am tired"; a statement of fact, not a magic incantation.

Do the same for every word in the list above. Add your own words to the list.

Another Word About Language

Most statements, in most languages, are actually metaphors. It is easy to mistake metaphor for fact. Here is an example. You are looking at a picture that shows a person and a hill. The person appears closer to the camera than the hill. We say "the person is in front of the hill." That statement is actually a metaphor. Hills do not have fronts and backs. It is just as appropriate to say the person is behind the hill as it is to say the person is in front of the hill. It would be more appropriate to say the hill is behind the person for people do have fronts and backs.

There is nothing wrong with metaphor. In fact, without it, language would be impossibly clumsy.

The problem arises when we all too easily confuse metaphor with fact.

A common example of confusing metaphor with fact is "higher consciousness." Do you have higher consciousness when you are flying in an airplane? How many people might say "yes"?

CPC217.u: Do not threaten other people's metaphors; for most monkeys, metaphors are facts. They are their identity and their identity is fragile.

CPC444.4: All identity is fragile. Avoid stepping on the glass at the next cocktail party.

YOU ARE YOUR OWN END. YOU ARE NOT THE MEANS TO ANYONE ELSE'S END.

CPC39.oto: However, it is wise to let others believe that you are a means to their ends.

IF YOU ARE NOT SELFISH YOU ARE WASTING YOUR LIFE.

Buy another copy of this book and send it to the President.

CPC-97.l: If you tell people you are selfish, they will not like you. Remember, words are more real than reality. Never let love take the place of power...but be sure to refer to power as "love." People use the word love when they are feeling weak. People do not use the word power when they are feeling strong...... Be as selfish as hell, but call yourself an altruist. Remember, you are always sacrificing yourself for the good of others.

CPC774: I was once told by a pompous, humble couple how intuitive their black maid was. What did I learn from this? Pay little and tell people they have secret powers. Remember, a maid is always a maid.

CPC=-09: The first label someone gives you is the label they will always believe.

CPC555.09: Labels are substitutes for reality. Learn to use them well and instill others to label you in the way you want. First impressions are difficult to overturn...... People do not like to admit they were wrong...and overturning labels threatens the primitive survival function of quick impressions.

CPC333.6: People are so much alike, it is a joke. However, they believe they are unique... Become a mind reader by telling them something they think you don't know about... Don't do this too often!!

CIVILIZATION IS NOTHING BUT A
DISGUISED FORM OF GENOCIDE

Despair Math

In this section I have provided a disparity coefficient meter as a method for finding out where you are *now*...... The items I have included are primary factors. I have left you the option to add a few of your own......

Answer these questions truthfully. That is, not what you want, believe you should have, or your personal ideal—but what you are *now*. This is your baseline......and base it must be......

I am not going to tell you what to do with your results until you are done taking the survey......

For each factor, circle one of the numbers below:

Intelligence

Low 1 2 3 4 5 6 7 High

How do you know your answer is factual?

How factual do you think it is?

Knowledge

Low 1 2 3 4 5 6 7 High

How do you know your answer is factual?

How factual do you think it is?

Wealth

Low 1 2 3 4 5 6 7 High

How do you know your answer is factual?

How factual do you think it is?

Sex

Low 1 2 3 4 5 6 7 High

How do you know your answer is factual?

How factual do you think it is?

Health

Low 1 2 3 4 5 6 7 High

How do you know your answer is factual?

How factual do you think it is?

Motivation

Low 1 2 3 4 5 6 7 High

How do you know your answer is factual?

How factual do you think it is?

Education
Low 1 2 3 4 5 6 7 High
How do you know your answer is factual?
How factual do you think it is?

Special Skills
Low 1 2 3 4 5 6 7 High
How do you know your answer is factual?
How factual do you think it is?

Attractiveness
Low 1 2 3 4 5 6 7 High
How do you know your answer is factual?
How factual do you think it is?

Social Skills
Low 1 2 3 4 5 6 7 High
How do you know your answer is factual?
How factual do you think it is?

Resistance to Anxiety and Fear
Low 1 2 3 4 5 6 7 High
How do you know your answer is factual?
How factual do you think it is?

Resistance to Depression
Low 1 2 3 4 5 6 7 High
How do you know your answer is factual?
How factual do you think it is?

Power
Low 1 2 3 4 5 6 7 High
How do you know your answer is factual?
How factual do you think it is?

Enlightened

   Low 1 2 3 4 5 6 7 High

How do you know your answer is factual?
How factual do you think it is?

Other

Use as many of these as you need

Now that you are finished, add all of the individual scores and come up with a total score. Divide this number by the number of questions you answered... Be sure to include the "other" category(s) if you used some of your own......

CPC549.oo: Support an altruistic cause. Spread rumors that jealous and greedy people are attempting to harm the cause... Always have someone to blame. Publicly give the credit for any successes to the efforts of the lowest workers.

Take a coffee break. Put this book down and come back in a day or two to finish the rest of the test.

How many people will follow my instructions? _____%

Circle the correct answer.
A. B. C. D. E. F. G. H.
None of the above

Stop, put the book away and come back later to finish the test......we are watching you!

Read "Terror Alert" and Then Take the Next Test.

Terror Alert

Checking the level of humanity—

Record an episode of the *Jerry Springer Show* and an episode of the evening news. What do they have in common? What are the differences? Be sure to compare the commercials. Keep in mind the assertion that the family is the ultimate line of protection. Against what? See the answer given earlier.

Now do the same with the *New York Times* and the *National Enquirer*.

Now take this version of the Despair Test but, this time, circle the number which represents what you WANT......

Circle one of the numbers below

Intelligence

Low 1 2 3 4 5 6 7 High

Is this desire highly probable?

How hard are you willing to work at achieving your goal or at
least approximating it?

What actions are you going to take?

Knowledge

Low 1 2 3 4 5 6 7 High

Is this desire highly probable?

How hard are you willing to work at achieving your goal or at
least approximating it?

What actions are you going to take?

Wealth

Low 1 2 3 4 5 6 7 High

Is this desire highly probable?

How hard are you willing to work at achieving your goal or at least approximating it?

What actions are you going to take?

Sex

Low 1 2 3 4 5 6 7 High

Is this desire highly probable?

How hard are you willing to work at achieving your goal or at least approximating it?

What actions are you going to take?

Health

Low 1 2 3 4 5 6 7 High

Is this desire highly probable?

How hard are you willing to work at achieving your goal or at least approximating it?

What actions are you going to take?

Motivation

Low 1 2 3 4 5 6 7 High

Is this desire highly probable?

How hard are you willing to work at achieving your goal or at least approximating it?

What actions are you going to take?

Education

Low 1 2 3 4 5 6 7 High

Is this desire highly probable?

How hard are you willing to work at achieving your goal or at least approximating it?

What actions are you going to take?

Special Skills

Low 1 2 3 4 5 6 7 High

Is this desire highly probable?

How hard are you willing to work at achieving your goal or at least approximating it?

What actions are you going to take?

Attractiveness

Low 1 2 3 4 5 6 7 High

Is this desire highly probable?

How hard are you willing to work at achieving your goal or at least approximating it?

What actions are you going to take?

Social Skills

Low 1 2 3 4 5 6 7 High

Is this desire highly probable?

How hard are you willing to work at achieving your goal or at least approximating it?

What actions are you going to take?

Resistance to Anxiety and Fear

Low 1 2 3 4 5 6 7 High

Is this desire highly probable?

How hard are you willing to work at achieving your goal or at least approximating it?

What actions are you going to take?

Resistance to Depression

Low 1 2 3 4 5 6 7 High

Is this desire highly probable?

How hard are you willing to work at achieving your goal or at least approximating it?

What actions are you going to take?

Power
> Low 1 2 3 4 5 6 7 High
Is this desire highly probable?
How hard are you willing to work at achieving your goal or at least approximating it?
What actions are you going to take?

Enlightened
> Low 1 2 3 4 5 6 7 High
Is this desire highly probable?
How hard are you willing to work at achieving your goal or at least approximating it?
What actions are you going to take?

Other
Use as many of these as you need.

Now that you are finished, add up all of the individual scores and come up with a total score. Divide this number by the number of questions answered... Be sure to include the "other" category(s) if you used some of your own......

Subtract the average score from the first survey from the average score on the second...... This number is your average Despair Coefficient.

You can also do this for each individual question to see where the greatest disparities occur.

EXERCISE INTERLUDE

Before we analyze the data, displease someone you really like, and please someone you really can't stand. Write down your actions and their reactions in your journal.

Back to Despair Math

Here's an example: what you are *now* has a mean score of 3 and what you *want* has a mean score of 2; your Despair Coefficient is -1. Thus you are a Christian, a liar, a fool, an idiot, a masochist or you can't read......

If your average score of what you have now is 3 and your mean score of what you want is 5, your Despair Coefficient is +2. This is your measurement of despair and your goal for improvement......

Now determine the Despair Coefficient for each individual question. Any question which has a difference score of +2 or more requires work... For example, on the intelligence issue, your "have now" score is 3 and what you want is 6; your Despair Coefficient is +3...... Ask yourself is this realistic and, if so, what might you have to do to approximate the score of 6? Remember, a 5 is all you really need... How do I know this?

From direct observation......

Below you will find a number of courses and other techniques for improving yourself...... But, for now, wait......and continue brainwashing yourself into unsanity.

Take a break and think about despair math. Is not this test something that people do automatically all the time? Are they not measuring themselves against some standard? You are to measure yourself against your own standards...... Keep in mind that words are more real than reality......

Interlude

Now, take a break, get on your dirty clothes and take a walk through a very wealthy neighborhood. If you don't want to wind up in jail, be sure to carry your ID, a credit card and $80.00 in tens, twenties and ones...... Be sure to remember or write down your thoughts and experiences......

Another Interlude

Once every three months attend a wedding, a funeral, or another social event of someone you don't know at all. Learn what you can about the people and the event and make up a story in case someone asks you why you are there...... If someone tries to throw you out, apologize, tell them you lost your family and were lonely...... See if they let you stay......

Nature Survey

(This survey is adapted from the work of W.H. Sheldon, M.D., Ph.D. Dr. Sheldon, although well respected in many areas of science, was frequently ostracized because of his focus on the inheritance of temperament. More recently, however, further research has tended to show that Dr. Sheldon was right after all.)

The following technique is one of the most important you will learn... It requires few direct questions, but instead utilizes observation and paying close attention to the conversation of other people. This will provide you with a powerful edge when you need one......

From memory, using the following scales, analyze someone you know very well. When you meet the person again compare your analysis with what you see.

This exam is designed to pick up on a person's fundamental nature. There are 9 points, so chose a number from 1 to 9. One is low and nine is high...

Set 1

A. Relaxed in Posture & Movement
   Dr. Hyatt's self rating is: 3

B. Assertive in Posture & Movement
   Dr. Hyatt's self rating is: 7

C. Restraint in Posture & Movement, Tightness
   Dr. Hyatt's self rating is: 2

Set 2

A. Love of Physical Comfort
   Dr. Hyatt's self rating is: 7

B. Love of Physical Adventure
   Dr. Hyatt's self rating is: 7

C. Over-reaction when stressed
   Dr. Hyatt's self rating is: 4

Set 3

A. Slow Reactions
   Dr. Hyatt's self rating is: 3

B. Energetic Reactions
   Dr. Hyatt's self rating is: 7

C. Overly Fast Reactions
   Dr. Hyatt's self rating is: 3

Set 4

A. Love of Eating
   Dr. Hyatt's self rating is: 7

B. Need and Enjoyment of Exercise
   Dr. Hyatt's self rating is: 4

C. Love of Privacy
   Dr. Hyatt's self rating is: 7

Set 5

A. Eating with others
   Dr. Hyatt's self rating is: 6

B. Love of Power
   Dr. Hyatt's self rating is: 9

C. Mental Over-intensity
   Dr. Hyatt's self rating is: 6

Set 6

A. Pleasure in relaxing after eating
   Dr. Hyatt's self rating is: 7

B. Love of Risk and Chance
   Dr. Hyatt's self rating is: 8

C. Secretiveness of Feeling, Emotional Restraint
   Dr. Hyatt's self rating is: 6

Set 7

A. Love of Polite Ceremony
   Dr. Hyatt's self rating is: 6

B. Bold Manner
   Dr. Hyatt's self rating is: 8

C. Self-Consciousness
   Dr. Hyatt's self rating is: 3

Set 8

A. Likes to be with people
   Dr. Hyatt's self rating is: 5

B. Courage for Combat
   Dr. Hyatt's self rating is: 7

C. Fear of people
   Dr. Hyatt's self rating is: 2

Set 9

A. Indiscriminate friendliness
   Dr. Hyatt's self rating is: 2

B. Competitive
   Dr. Hyatt's self rating is: 5

C. Inhibited Socially
   Dr. Hyatt's self rating is: 3

Set 10

A. Need for Affection and Approval
   Dr. Hyatt's self rating is: 4

B. Callousness
   Dr. Hyatt's self rating is: 6

C. Likes routines
   Dr. Hyatt's self rating is: 3

Set 11

A. Orientation to People
   Dr. Hyatt's self rating is: 3

B. Not Claustrophobic
   Dr. Hyatt's self rating is: 7

C. Fear of open spaces
  Dr. Hyatt's self rating is: 1

Set 12

A. Evenness of emotional reaction
  Dr. Hyatt's self rating is: 6

B. Not Squeamish
  Dr. Hyatt's self rating is: 7

C. Unpredictability of attitude
  Dr. Hyatt's self rating is: 6

Set 13

A. Tolerance
  Dr. Hyatt's self rating is: 4

B. Unrestrained voice
  Dr. Hyatt's self rating is: 6

C. Dislikes Noisy Situations
  Dr. Hyatt's self rating is: 6

Set 14

A. Complacency
  Dr. Hyatt's self rating is: 3

B. Indifference to pain
  Dr. Hyatt's self rating is: 6

C. Hypersensitivity to pain
  Dr. Hyatt's self rating is: 2

Set 15

A. Deep sleep
  Dr. Hyatt's self rating is: 4

B. Requires little sleep
  Dr. Hyatt's self rating is: 6

C. Poor sleep habits, chronic fatigue
  Dr. Hyatt's self rating is: 4

Set 16
A. Average appearance (for age)
Dr. Hyatt's self rating is: 8

B. Over maturity of appearance
Dr. Hyatt's self rating is: 3

C. Youthful manner and appearance
Dr. Hyatt's self rating is: 4

Set 17
A. Clear communication of feelings
Dr. Hyatt's self rating is: 7

B. Free body movement
Dr. Hyatt's self rating is: 7

C. Poor communication of feeling
Dr. Hyatt's self rating is: 3

Set 18
A. Relaxation—social communication when drinking
Dr. Hyatt's self rating is: 7

B. Assertiveness while drinking
Dr. Hyatt's self rating is: 3

C. Resistance to alcohol
Dr. Hyatt's self rating is: 7

Set 19
A. Need of people when stressed
Dr. Hyatt's self rating is: 4

B. Need of action when stressed
Dr. Hyatt's self rating is: 7

C. Need of solitude when stressed
Dr. Hyatt's self rating is: 7

Set 20
A. Orientation toward childhood, fantasy and/or family
Dr. Hyatt's self rating is: 2

B. Orientation toward goals and activities of youth
   Dr. Hyatt's self rating is: 5

C. Orientation toward the later periods of life
   Dr. Hyatt's self rating is: 4

What does this mean? Each of the 20 sets contains three descriptive factors: A, B, and C. Add all the A scores and divide by 20; do the same with the B scores and the C scores.

For example I will analyze myself.

A score is: 97/20=4.85
B score is: 125/20=6.25
C score is: 80/20=4.00

The scores must be arranged with A first, B second, and C third. My overall profile is A=4.85; B=6.25; C=4.00.

Check my math, please.

Superficially these scores say that my basic orientation toward life is activity, accomplishment, and aggression. This is revealed by my B Score, my highest score.

Next I enjoy the physical comforts of life, and can be self-indulgent. This is revealed by my A Score, the next highest score.

Finally, while at times I am introverted, my overall style is that of an aggressive extrovert...... This is revealed by my C score, my lowest score.

This is my basic nature......and any attempts to restrict me would be met with aggression, rebellion and direct resistance. It also tells us that I would get along better with people who were higher in A and B scores than C scores. In passing, I would say that I intensely dislike people with extreme C scores......and enjoy people who like moderate, occasional social gatherings, particularly if it leads to accomplishing a goal. From this information and what you can gather from this survey determine what tactics you would use to manipulate me to do what you want.

A lot more information can be gleaned from this evaluation; for example, by comparing the magnitude of differences between scores, by looking at the average score for each variable, and by comparing the average score for each variable to each individual score from each set...... Its power is endless...... But will you learn how to use this power?

One very powerful quality of this method is that you don't have to ask questions; you can observe and listen and find out a lot about a person...... This will allow you to adjust your tactics when you interact with others.

This is one of the most important techniques... I can't overstress this. It can be used to select mates and friends, to find latent enemies, and to get along with almost anyone...... It is powerful and has been condemned by society—particularly by the liberal academic community—because it emphasizes innate tendencies and individual differences. And, after all, aren't we all "equal"?

Now, using the same scales, analyze someone you just met...... Wait a month and analyze them again...... What are the differences?

Analyze the President
Analyze your parents.
Analyze your mate
Analyze your children.
Analyze Adolf Hitler.
Analyze Jesus and Buddha.
Analyze Zehm Alohim.
Analyze yourself.
Analyze your friends
Analyze an enemy and develop tactics to conquer or influence
    them.
Have someone who knows you well analyze you.

The First Thirty Minutes

These are the most important minutes of the day, the first 30 minutes after you wake up. Keep track of all emotions, feelings and, in particular, thoughts which "pop" into your mind. Write these down no matter how silly they may seem. After the day is over, go back over them. See what you can make of them. After a week go over them again and see what theme is developing. After a month do it again. Write a paragraph containing no moralization's—that is, no good's or bad's—describing the themes you have discovered.

Model of People

LIMITATION

IS SECURITY

a. 90% of all humans are simply machines, regardless of wealth, education, etc. They are "DNA essentials"—DEAD ENDERS.

Make a list of ten people you know or have heard of. Remember, this list includes most people that most people admire or think are great.

b. About 9.5% (that is, less than 10%) are marginal; that includes many great people as well as the worst criminals and derelicts. They are DNA options. This is the group "we are in." This is an assumption, of course.

Make a list of ten people you either know or have heard of.

c. About 0.5% (one-half of one percent or less) are the truly great ones; some are hidden and others are in the open. These are DNA gambles—or "errors."

Make a list of ten people you either know or, most likely, have heard of.

P.S. By knowing your heroes you will know yourself. This can be a great embarrassment......

Some of my heroes are:

F.W.N.
S.F.
W.H.S.
G. Patton
Field Marshall Rommel
Bozo

Dr. Hyatt's Demands

You would think that Humans might spend their time overcoming death, disease, stupidity. Dr. Lindner said that in the mid-1950's and Dr. Leary picked up the bandwagon. Now it is our turn, doing something—any something—every day to demolish this morass of human pollution.

If you spend your time working like a fool—believing, romanticizing, breeding, nesting and digesting—you deserve whatever happens to you. If this is your "choice," please leave the class.

Dr. Dad and staff have prepared a list of course-exercises. I use the phrases course-exercises and exercise-courses to convey the idea of the seriousness of this program and training. I am presenting as complete a program as possible on short notice. However, I expect only a few will attempt the program, let alone complete it. The modern world contains very few who think of anything but social status, sex and fulfilling their biologic imperatives.

CPC111.8: Help people use what is natural for them to keep them in their place. Help people get married, buy houses, shop and have lots of children.

All pleasure and all pain are brain phenomena. Here is an assumption-blaster: did you ever hand in a paper or take a test, get an A grade, and feel bad because you wanted a C grade?

How about the reverse?

If you have ever seen a child who did not get bored when he did not have something to do, then you have seen a hibernating bear in people-clothing. Human beings are accomplishment creatures. Even when we sleep, we accomplish through dreaming. Vegetables don't accomplish. That is why we refer to not accomplishing anything as "vegging out."

CPC874.aa: Help people accomplish what they will do anyway. They will always be indebted to you. Help them find a secure job, help them get laid, invite them to parties, help them get married, help them have children, help them buy a house, help them have a barbecue.

> Help them do what is normal for a talking monkey......
> Remember, words are more real than reality...... Help them
> be as common as they are and tell them they are doing
> right, being good, being profound. Tell them about their
> secret talents......

To be human is to accomplish. To accomplish is to think. Computers simply repeat what they have been programmed to do. People who simply repeat what they have been told to do are animated computers.

Learning takes effort. Applying what you learn takes even more effort.

Accomplishment takes effort. Learning is an accomplishment. To be other than an animated computer or a monkey in cloth is to constantly expand your learning and, more importantly, your power.

Some of these course-exercises can be taken at junior or senior colleges, either for credit or audited. You could simply go to various university bookstores, look at the courses you need to take, and buy the books. However, you must be disciplined.

Other course-exercises can be taken on the web: videos, books and the like. Still others can be taken at private institutions or by requesting manuals and ads from corporations.

You can learn to use automatic weapons at some gun ranges.

Some of these courses can only be taught by Dr. Hyatt or his associates. For those that wish it—and can afford it—papers, developing ideas, etc. can be sent to the Dr. for his comments, evaluation and recording.

You must have money to pay for these courses and exercises. How you accomplish this is your business. Some of the training will be difficult or almost impossible to find, but this is your quest and problem. We have provided some references; however, they are incomplete, leaving enough room for you to find your own.

For a fee we will provide guidance. (PayPal, Cashier's Checks, Cash and Money Orders get immediate attention; personal checks must clear the bank first.)

Our motto is "no excuses." PAY NOW—JUST DO IT—NOW!

P.S.: There is a lot to learn and, more importantly, a lot to apply. Choose what is best for you and don't allow the number of courses to distract you...... It was designed to discourage you.........

If and when you have completed these exercise-courses successfully, you will be have earned the right to call yourself more than human; thus, you can stop being ashamed of being an *involuntary* member of the human race.

You will be better trained and more powerful than most. You will be able to go anywhere and do anything you decide to do.

How long will this take? As long as necessary. The definition of "work" in economics is: something done as a means to an end. The definition of "recreation" is: something done as an end in itself. **Self-improvement through study violates the standard of economics. It is work in that it is a means to an end and it is recreation in that it is an end in itself.**

Interlude

"Could the young but realize how soon they will become bundles of habits, they would give more heed to their conduct while in the plastic state. We are spinning our own fates, good or evil, and never to be undone. Every smallest stroke of virtue or of vice leaves its never so little scar. The drunken Rip Van Winkle, in Jefferson's play, excuses himself for every fresh dereliction by saying, 'I won't count this time.' Well! he may well not count it, and a kind Heaven may not count it; but it is being counted none the less. Down among his nerve-cells and fibers the molecules are counting it, registering and storing it up to be used against him when the next temptation comes. Nothing we ever do, in strict scientific literalness, is wiped out. Of course this has its good side as well as its bad one. As we become permanent drunkards by so many separate drinks, so we become saints in the moral, and authorities and experts in the practical scientific spheres, by so many separate acts and hours of work. Let no youth have any anxiety about the upshot of his education, whatever the line of it may be. If he keeps faithfully busy each hour of the working-day, he may safely leave the final result to itself. He can with perfect certainty count on waking up some fine morning, to find himself one of the competent ones of his generation, in whatever pursuit he may have singled out."

— William James, *Principles of Psychology*

Brain Change Willed

When you study something new, your brain actually makes new connections and grows in size. The increase in size is tiny, but the increase in new connections is massive. New connections don't develop instantaneously, they take time to grow. *We want to emphasize that the right way to learn new material is to read the book at least three times. The first time just read it straight through. You may well not understand much at all; it does not matter. Just keep reading.*

The second time through, it will mostly make a lot of sense. The third time through you will understand and likely learn the material. Those three readings give your brain time to grow those new connections and set them in place. The first reading is hard. The second reading is interesting. The third reading is fun.

All power to the brain. The creator of gods, ghosts, myths, fantasies, knowledge, beauty, and reference.

These exercise-courses will not make you a specialist but rather a generalist—although you may choose to specialize in as many areas as you wish. They are not designed to get you a job, but to change you in a radical way and become someone you won't recognize.

Manual III

The No-Where University
Sometimes Called P.U.

Dr. Hyatt, Spanking Master
Dr. Willis, President
Zehm Alohim, Student Affairs
Banker Jew, Finance
Missy, Studio Director
S. Jason Black, Cartoons
Nick Tharcher, Publishing
Madame X, Sex Education
H. Himmler Jr., Student Selections
Big Dave, Provost Marshal and armorer

P.U.

Your Local Academics!

The model of transformation presented here is based on the old Saracen system of education. If a student wanted to learn and a teacher wanted to teach, they would come to an arrangement. The teacher was not licensed by either the State or the Church, and there were no entrance requirements other than those agreed upon. If the student and teacher become unhappy with each other, the student would simply find another teacher or vice versa. If and when the student was satisfied with what he wanted to learn he would simply leave. The student would pay for what he wanted and then went on to the next teacher or area of interest.

Homes were often used as classrooms as were rented facilities; sometimes these would grow into small communities of learning where services required by the student—lodging, food, etc.—were simply paid for. Over time, some of these small centers grew into profound centers of learning, yet there was no or little formality and no state interference.

In the final analysis, the proof of the student's knowledge was his ability, and not degrees, certificates, grades or licenses. This form of education is, of course, unacceptable in today's world of point-and-click mentality.

IF YOU NEED TO BE FORGIVEN, THEN YOU WILL STEAL AGAIN

Terror Alert

The Catalog for the Psychopath

> ## EXERCISE 5.34
>
> **What is "Guilt Free Living"? Define it as a Christian. Define it as a Jew. Define it as a Politician. Define it as a Psychopath.**

Fundamentally there are three types of guilt. We call them:

1. Existential: That which comes from the very fact of existence. You exist so you do not want anyone to steal your property or to hurt you. Thus, we do not steal other people's property, nor do we initiate physical violence. We assert that violating these principles can, and should, result in guilt—existential guilt.

2. Biblical/Social: Except for existential guilt (which both bibles and society generally include in their babble), the remainder is utter nonsense and designed to tame and control. To find examples of this type of guilt thumb a bible or a law book.

3. Developmental: Those specific stupidities that derive from the process of being raised. For example, your parents wanted you to be a dentist and you became a pilot.

Sometimes I collapse the three categories into two: existential and neurotic.

Guilt has two feelings associated with it: fear and self-hate......
Fear relates to punishment and self-hate *is* self-punishment.

When you feel guilt whose origins are biblical/social or developmental, you are weakened. This is their purpose—to weaken you.

When you feel guilty, immediately ignore the associated thoughts; instead, associate an image which gives you pleasure.

Instead of focusing on the feelings or the associated thoughts, force yourself to focus on the pleasurable image...... In time you will be mostly guilt free. But remember, you must practice and not allow yourself to entertain the associated bad feelings or thoughts. Do not argue with yourself whether you are guilty or not—just force yourself to practice.

Before you can do this you will have to find life experiences that gave you pleasure, or invent an image that you think will give you pleasure.

Since a person's identity partially consists of guilt feelings and all it entails, as you begin to become guilt free you may feel anxiety. This is natural as you are re-constructing yourself—which means you do not feel like your usual self. This is not the problem that many professionals would like you to believe. It is a sign of self-empowerment.

CPC YYY: Dysfunctional self-interest: People who are motivated by self-interest are the smartest people to work with; however, a large group who *claim* self interest are actually highly dysfunctional...... Their self-interest is motivated by intense inferior feelings so they are primarily self-destructive and dangerous......

Undoing Yourself:
Some Important Terms
to Keep in Mind

a. Beliefs

Beliefs are unquestioned assumptions (see below) which are often spoken aloud and practiced day-to-day in your everyday life.

b. Behavior-Habits

This is what you do day-to-day like an machine weaves clothes. It is the way you put on clothes, address your boss, talk to your husband, how you cook, etc.

c. Attitudes

These are points of view similar to beliefs but believed by the talking monkey to have been thought out. Most of these are peer group and media generated.

d. Assumptions

Assumptions are neither good nor bad, but simply unexplored belief patterns which have not been questioned rationally or empirically. Most of what we do, belief and say are based on false assumptions. Find all your assumptions and question them with the utmost cruelty.

e. Mommy and Daddy

These are the two primates who you imprinted on. They taught you how to think, act and what to believe long before you could question their assumptions or even acquired language. You learned to imitate them, to rebel blindly against them, and your psychological development was primarily dependent on them.

They, of course, are simply talking monkeys reflecting the non-sense belief and history inculcated in them. Study them as talking monkeys; drop the label parents, replace it with talking monkeys.

Some Psychology Terms

a. Greed

The horror of helplessness. An out-of-control state of the "soul" that makes you a victim. Greed is very different from getting what you want.

b. Fear

Something often real, like an approaching car. At times, an almost paralyzing emotion. More often than not, fear is induced by the anticipation of punishment and is the result of early learning and an undisciplined imagination.

c. Anxiety

An anticipatory response, more often than not irrational. The feeling of melting away, of disappearing, of falling apart.

d. Frustration

Being thwarted in getting what you want when you want. Often frustration leads to aggression and/or depression instead of productive efforts to get around obstacles.

Terms for you to define:

aggression
depression
perversions
shame
guilt
hostility
humiliation

self-destructive and other destructive behavior.
addictions
neurotic
psychotic
sociopathic behavior
personality disorders......

The Courses

Keep in mind that—
The psychopath is an individual with maximum flexibility. He responds to the reality of things, not the cultural fiction; however, he uses fiction to accomplish his will.

He thinks for himself and reaches his own conclusions. That means he is a threat to the herd. The herd hates the independent thinker. The herd attempts to destroy the different.

You are a threat to the herd. They will try to destroy you. At all times you must be prepared for their attack. Self protection is the first law of life.

Study this book over and over to learn how to protect yourself and increase your power and quality of life.

The titles and authors listed in this section are mostly accurate. Some, however, may not be, either deliberately or due to error. Live with it.

Disclaimer: These courses are not intended to make you into a criminal or to encourage you to commit any illegal acts.

Logic and Rational Process

a. Basic book on reasoning
   — *The Art of Reasoning*, Kelly
   — *Post Modern Logic*, Negoita

b. Symbolic logic
   — *How to Prove It*, Velleman

c. Socio-linguistics
   — *That's Not What I Meant: How Conversational Style Makes or Breaks Relationships*, Tannen
   — *You Just Don't Understand: Men and Women in Conversation*, Tannen

Irrational Processes

a. Psychic powers

b. Intuition
c. Imagination
d. Reading
   — *Pacts with the Devil*, Black & Hyatt
   — *Lies, Lies and More Lies*, Hyatt

> CPC-93X: Masturbation is pleasure without cost. So how might you make people pay?

Statistical Truth

The world as seen through inferential statistics. Study chi square and apply it. Study the following to learn how statistics and classifications are used.
   — *Diagnostic and Statistical Manual of Mental Disorders (DSM-IV-TR)*, American Psychiatric Association

Structures of Economics and Institutions

a. Austrian economics
   — *Economics in One Lesson*, Hazlitt
   — *Essentials of Economics: A Brief Survey of Principles and Policies*, Ballve
   — *The Law*, Bastiat
   — *Economic Fallacies*, Bastiat

b. Banking
   — *A Short Course in International Payments: How to Use Letters of Credit, D/P and D/a Terms, Prepayment, Credit, and Cyber-payments in International Transactions*, Hinkelman
   — *Money, Credit, and Commerce*, Marshall; *Financial Institutions, Markets, and Money*, Kidwell

c. Agencies
   — *Bureaucracy*, von Mises
   — *Unbridled Power: Inside the Secret Culture of the IRS*, Davis
   — *Innocent Casualties: The FDA's War Against Humanity*, Feuer

d. Insurance
— *Insurance for Dummies*, Hungelmann
— *Theory and Practice of Insurance*, Outreville

e. Business
— *Capitalism and the Historians*, Hayek
— *The Art of Negotiating*, Nierenber
— *Secrets of Closing Sales*, Roth & Alexander
— *Guerrilla Marketing Weapons: 100 Affordable Marketing Methods for Maximizing Profits from Your Small Business*, Levinson

f. Equity and commodity investing
There are many good books in this area. You should learn about: all the kinds of trades that can be made in a stock market, how the commodities markets work (including the types of trades), and the different types of mutual funds (including international funds).

Disguise and Deception

a. Make-up classes
1. Face
— *Emotions Revealed: Recognizing Faces and Feelings to Improve Communication and Emotional Life*, Ekman
2. Body
— *Conquering Deception*, Nance
— *I know what You're Really Thinking: Reading Body Language Like a Trial Lawyer*, Mogil
3. Movement
— *Body Learning: An Introduction to the Alexander Technique*, Gelb and Huxley
— *Constructive Awareness: Alexander Technique and the Spiritual Quest*, McGowan

b. Acting—The Essentials
Take acting classes at local colleges or workshops.

c. Building your own identity
1. Names and their effects

2. Clothes and their effects

d. Attractiveness
   1. Using body assets
   2. Social skills
   3. Dancing
   4. Eating in all environments

e. Propaganda and Communication
   1. Religion: Christianity, Judaism, Islam, Buddhism, Hinduism, Occultism, Voodoo; become expert at one or more
   2. Ideophilia
   3. Advertisement and marketing
   4. Principles of speech
   5. Argumentation and assumptions

f. Stereotyping
   1. Imaging people
   2. Knowing how you and others are seen.
   — *Body Image: A Handbook of Theory, Research, and Clinical Practice,* Cash and Pruzinsky
   — *Appearance Is Everything: The Hidden Truth Regarding Your Appearance Discrimination,* Jeffes

Philosophy Or...
Homeland Security?

Not For Sale
in California

ALL PHILOSOPHY EVENTUALLY
BECOMES A DICTATORSHIP

The best psychopath is the one most free of thinking errors. The study of philosophy is one of the best ways to learn to spot errors in thinking in yourself and others. Every one of the philosophers listed below has made major contributions to the psychopath's life and every one has errors. Your job is to study them and then find at least some of the errors. For each philosopher, read something of his or a summary of his thinking and then read a book of criticisms.

Start with an introductory course in philosophy at your local university or junior college. All philosophers are bigots for their own system. The psychopath is a bigot for the system that benefits his own life. The law of the psychopath is: how does this help me get what I want in life.

> **Introduction:** *Introduction to Philosophical Analysis,* John Hospers [try to get the 2nd edition; if it is not available then the current 4th edition]
> **Aristotle:** *The Nicomachean Ethics*
> **Plato:** *The Republic*
> **Marcus Aurelius:** *Meditations*
> **Spinoza:** *Treatise on the Emendation of the Intellect*
> **Mill:** *The Logic of the Moral Sciences*
> **Hume:** *An Inquiry Concerning Human Understanding; Dialogues and Natural History of Religion*
> **Locke:** *The Second Treatise on Civil Government*
> **Nietzsche:** *Nietzsche, Philosopher, Psychologist, Antichrist,* Walter Kaufmann
> **Rand:** *The Fountainhead; Atlas Shrugged*
> **Blanshard:** *Reason and Analysis*

Interpersonal Relationships

> a. How to win friends and influence people
> — *How to Win Friends and Influence People,* Carnegie
> — *Leadership 101: What Every Leader Needs to Know,* Maxwell

---

CPC0379.a: People are always looking for flaws in other people. Be sure you let them see a few......however, just in small things.

> b. Shame & Guilt
> — *Shame and Guilt,* Dearing

— *Shame and Guilt: Masters of Disguise*, Middelton-Moz

c. Sex: Exotic and Normal
— *Passionate Marriage: Love, Sex, and Intimacy in Emotionally Committed Relationships*, Schnarch
— *Kama Sutra of Sexual Positions: The Tantric Art of Love*, Stubbs
— *Secrets of Western Tantra*, Hyatt
— *Sex Magick, Tantra & Tarot*, Hyatt

Investments

a. Basics, stocks, bonds, real estate
— *Study Guide for Trading for a Living: Psychology, Trading Tactics, Money Management*, Elder
— *Come Into My Trading Room: A Complete Guide to Trading*, Elder
— *International Tax Havens Guide: The Professional's Source for Offshore Investment Information*, Spitz

b. Exotics, diamonds, rare metals, rarities
Anything that exists can be, is, or will be a collectable. Psychopaths collect for the fun of it or the profit of it or both. The basic law of collectibles is: the knowledgeable will exploit the novice. Your choice: exploit or be exploited. Write in your journal any rational reason why you should not exploit. Prove it from first principles.

Computers

Rather than recommend books in this area, we would recommend that you take courses at your local junior college or the adult extension division of your local university. You do need to understand the technology of computers in general (e.g. what is 1394, what is a "front end bus", etc. You may want to take courses in various common computer programs, but mostly they are too slow and you can get all your need from books. You also want to take one or two programming classes. This is not so much a way for you to become a programmer as it is a way for you to learn to think in a very linear logical fashion. Learning to use the web you can learn from any friend and a little experience.

a. What is behind the screen
b. Basics of programming
c. Using the Internet

Fundamentals of Physics and Chemistry

a. Basic chemical compounds
b. How the physical world works
The best possible way to learn about the 'fundamentals of physics and chemistry' is to take a course in each or a course in 'the physical sciences' at a local university, junior college, or an internet course. More and more courses like this are available over the internet, developed by universities. Note that you are not going for any degree, but for knowledge.

Principles of Pain and Pleasure

a. Basic anatomy and physiology
Choose a basic college text book. You don't want to get something like Gray's Anatomy, that degree of knowledge is unnecessary. Nor do you want to get a medical text on physiology. You want a basic introductory book, perhaps one used in courses for nurses.

b. Neurology, brain
  — *Cognitive Neuroscience, the Biology of the Mind,* Gazzaniga and Ivry and Mangum
  — *Psychological Science,* Gazzaniga and Heatherton
  — *How the Mind Works,* Pinker

Medical Knowledge

a. First Aid (Wounds, injuries and illness)
First aid can be learned from a Red Cross course. The general knowledge of medicine can be obtained reading (at least twice) any current book on home medicine.

b. Preventive medicine
As a practicing psychopath, you are the ultimate decider of medical advice. Yes, your doctor likely knows more than you do about the medical

problem (but not always). But if you have a medical condition, it is your life that is affected and your doctor is an advisor, not a controller.

c. Massage

If you have a massage school locally, you can take a course there. If not, here is a book: Basic Clinical Massage Therapy: Integrating Anatomy and Treatment, Clay and Pounds

d. Drugs and Their Effects
   1. Pain
   2. Stimulants
   3. Psychedelics
   4. Basic survival drugs and body systems

Language Skills

a. Basics
b. Creative writing
c. Scientific writing

All of the above can be learned at your local university or junior college. There are many books on basics, creative writing, and scientific writing. Scientific writing can be studied just by reading a couple of dozen articles in scientific periodicals from different disciplines. You don't care about the content because that is for other like scientists—you care about the style of writing.

Children

Children are not possessions. they are potential. leave them alone to develop that potential. children do not need strictness nor indulgence, they need knowledge. Be a COACH and an EXAMPLE, not a cop or a dripping breast.

    a. Basic principles of child development
    — *The Essential Piaget,* Piaget, et al.
    — *A Secure Base: Parent-Child Attachment and Healthy Human Development,* Bowlby

     b. Child cognitive development and the cognitive world of the child.

— *How to Raise a Brighter Child: The Case for Early Learning*, Beck

— *How Children Learn*, Holt

— *Home Learning Year by Year: How to Design a Homeschool Curriculum from Preschool Through High School*, Rupp

— *The Well-Trained Mind: A Guide to Classical Education at Home*, Wise and Bauer

   c. Getting along with children

— *Between Parent and Child*, Ginott

— *Your Child Is a Person: A Psychological Approach to Parenthood Without Guilt*, Chess, et al.

Politics and Authorities

   a. Law

     1. Fundamentals of criminal law

     2. Criminal justice system

     3. Fundamentals of civil law

     4. Dealing with authorities

   b. Forensics

     1. Physical

     2. Psychological

     3. Profiling

     4. Passive and active interrogation

   c. Tyrants

— *The Origins of Totalitarianism*, Arendt

— *The Road to Serfdom*, Hayek

— *Modern Tyrants: The Power and Prevalence of Evil in Our Age*, Chirot

Personality Types

— *The Biological Basis of Personality*, Eysenck

Freud

— *Psychopathology of Everyday Life*, Freud

— *New Introductory Lectures*, Freud

Jung's Thinking, Intuition, Feeling and Physical Types
— *Psychological Types,* Jung

Jung Discovering the Archetypes

Physical

a. Physical Conditioning
— Gymnastics
— Weight training
— Stamina
— Weight and body fat control

b. Sports
Become average or superior in at least two games (e.g., golf, racquet-ball, polo, tennis)

c. Hand-to-Hand Combat
— Boxing
— Marital arts
— Your choice

d. Use of Small Arms
— Pistol
— Rifle
— Automatic weapons
— Batons
— Knives
— Normal objects

e. Survival
— Jungle
— Desert
— Mountain
— Ocean
— City
— Sensory deprivation

EXERCISE 47.4

For one month act like a U.S. Marine boot one day each week.

---

f. Acts of Danger
— Sky diving
— Scuba diving
— Motorcycle Sports
— Electives

History Of Warfare

Reading
— *History of the Peloponnesian War*, Thucydides

— *The Art of War*, Griffith
— *The Art of Strategy: A New Translation of Sun Tzu's Classic The Art of War*, Sun-Tzu
— *Makers of Modern Strategy from Machiavelli to the Nuclear Age*, Paret

Military Tactics and Strategies

What are they? Set up a defensive system; then overcome it.

Intelligence

a. Gathering of intelligence
b. Normal sources
c. Observational and deductive sources

Electronic Devices

a. Voice
b. Polygraph
c. Camera
d. Telephone, radio, TV
e. GPS
f. Biofeedback

Security Systems

a. Electronic
b. Mechanical

Transportation

a. Become competent at one or more of the following: flying, sailing and driving
b. Knowledge of the others; computer models may be used for two, but one must be hands on

Mental Discipline

a. Hypnosis, Meditation and Pain Deflection
1. Memory

2. Manipulation
3. Self control
4. Reading
— *Monsters & Magical Sticks: There's No Such Thing as Hypnosis?*, Heller
— *Undoing Yourself With Energized Meditation and Other Devices*, Hyatt
b. Behavior Modification
1. Operant
2. Classical
3. Emotional

Language Skills

a. Excellent use of one foreign language
b. Average use of another
c. *The Language Instinct*, Pinker
d. *Women, Fire and Dangerous Things*, Lakoff

Fundamentals of Gambling

a. Poker
b. Casino games
c. Polite games

General Information

a. History of Egypt, Greece and Rome
b. Automobiles
c. Art
d. Astrology
e. Movies
f. Books: become conversant in at least two periods (e.g., American literature of the 1920s; French literature of the *fin-de-siècle*; German literature of the mid-1800s)
g. News

Mechanics and Artistry

a. Auto or other
b. Casting jewelry or other
c. Painting
d. Poetry
e. Carpentry
f. Music

Independent Study

a. Course—exercises you choose.
b. Course—exercises that Dr. Hyatt and staff develop for you —once we know you well

The Study and Performance of Ritual

a. Catholic Mass
b. Gnostic Mass
c. The Black Mass
d. Reading
— *The Complete Golden Dawn System of Magic,* Regardie
— *Condensed Chaos,* Hine
— *PsyberMagick,* Carroll
— *The ChaoChamber System* (CD and booklet), Brown

A Parting Shot

Anger is a creative emotion.

Bad things will happen.

De-automate your robot thoughts.

Do the unexpected—surprise yourself.

Take risks; stop self-defeating behavior.

Find and identify in detail your present beliefs and robotic behavior.

Burn out repetitive automatic thoughts.

Treat your beliefs and stupid behavior as if they were on trial… Use your mind to convict them.

Substitute Power Behavior for Stupid Behavior.

ReWork Old Memories—know the past—forget the past.

Appendices:
The Sado-Masochism of Self-Healing

Appendix I

A Few Useful Teaching Tools
by Nicholas Tharcher

The following is a short, semi-random list of books, movies and events which we like for various reasons and which the aspiring or practicing Toxick Magician might find useful to study. Each has its own unique quality and some may have no value to you at all; we may even have included some as ringers.

In many cases these works provide information about attitudes and occasionally about techniques (martial arts movies can be useful in both regards). Only in a few cases, however, do we recommend the work unreservedly: often the amount of useful information varies tremendously. Some (like *The Thomas Crown Affair* and *Point Break)* are excellent portrayals of the psychopath from beginning to end. Others (like *Thelma and Louise* are more limited—in our view it was rather so-so until the end), In some the psychopath-protagonists are highly limited by the circumstances of their social environment (e.g., in *Goodfellas* the full expression of psychopathy was limited—not because of the wider external society, but because of the more limited society of a gang with its own rules.)

You may find it useful to consider some of our criteria for *excluding* some titles: many potential candidates were left off the list because the characters come off as too pathetic, or as socialized/moralized, or as driven only by outside forces or as "crazy."

As we were putting this list together we noted that many examples fell into certain distinct categories (though a few seem to defy categorization—*Being There* is a good example). The main categories, however, seemed to be 1) Vengeance, 2) Obsession, 3) Expressing the "Will to Power," and 4) Doing Your Own "True Will." We also noted another category which we could only describe as "Boring": they include almost all political movies; e.g., *Nixon*.

For a while we felt surprised that we found so few candidates in certain groups, notably Science Fiction and War Movies. Perhaps that's because the former group seems mostly concerned with the improvement of the species (though frankly we can't think of many that succeed even minimally: when Captain Kirk says, "I'm from Iowa; I only *work* in outer space," he seems to make the point most eloquently) and War Movies seem focused on an area which is inherently tied to accepted social values.

One may argue that some titles do not belong on the list at all; on the other hand, one may argue that we missed obvious and significant works. We certainly won't argue about that.

Here's our list:

Above Suspicion
And Then There Were None
Arsenic and Old Lace
Assassins
Atlas Shrugged (not done as a movie—exceptional!!)
Being There
Butch Cassidy and the Sundance Kid (excellent!)
Cape Fear (both versions have their points)
Captain's Paradise, The
Count of Monte Christo, The
Death Wish I
Death Wish II
Dogs of War, The
Donny Brasco
Falling Down

First Blood (Rambo 1)
Fountainhead, The (excellent book; fair movie)
Getaway, The (both the Steve McQueen/Ali MacGraw and the Alec
    Baldwin/Kim Basinger versions have their points though we
    prefer the former)
Godfather, The (especially the first one)
Goodfellas
Great Impostor, The (based on a true story)
In the Line of Fire
Kelly's Heroes (one of the few war films on our list)
King of New York, The
Magic Christian, The
Mechanic, The (excellent!)
Moby Dick (contrast the obsessional qualities with *The Searchers)*
Nevada Smith
One-Eyed Jacks
Our Man Flint
Point Break (excellent!!)
Point of No Return (excellent!)
Ransom
Road House
Rough Cut
Runaway Train (excellent film, terrible title)
Scarface (Pacino version)
School for Scoundrels
Sea Wolf, The
Serial Mom
Shawshank Redemption, The
Shogun (portrays an entire culture which essentially held
    psychopathy as a value; an historical rarity)
Silence of the Lambs (classic!)
Specialist, The
Sting, The
Tequila Sunrise
Thelma & Louise (particularly at the end)
Thomas Crown Affair, The (1968 version; excellent!)
To Catch a Thief

Usual Suspects, The
Wild Geese (but not *Wild Geese II)*

Many martial arts film (for technique and attitude)

Another useful classification we noted includes training devices which help illustrate *how the system really works.* Most of these examples are from "real life" and are far from exhaustive. It seems that in this classification, "fact" can be far more educational than fiction.

Movies

And Justice for All
Nixon

Other Stuff

- Any newspaper, any TV/Radio news program, any day: (to quote Walter Kaufman, scholar and translator of Friedrich Nietzsche and Martin Buber):

  Mundus vult decipi: The world wants to be deceived. The truth is too complex and frightening; the taste for the truth is an acquired taste that few acquire.

  Not all deceptions are palatable. Untruths are too easy to come by, too quickly exploded and ephemeral to give lasting comfort. *Mundus vult decipi*; but there is a hierarchy of deceptions.

  Near the bottom of the ladder is journalism: a steady stream of irresponsible distortions that most people find refreshing, though on the morning after, or at least within a week, will be stale and flat.
  — Prologue to Martin Buber's *I and Thou*

- Any high school or college text on history, economics or any of the so-called "social sciences".
- The O.J. Simpson trial (with unlimited resources available to both the prosecution and defense, this can only be considered

the ideal example of American justice at its very, very best; contrast with the movie *And Justice for All*).

- The "McMartin Preschool Trial" in the 1980's (and many of the other witch hunts that followed); also done as a movie by HBO, *Indictment: The McMartin Preschool Trial.*
- The President William Jefferson Clinton impeachment and "trial".
- The Chicago 7 trial in 1969–1970 resulting from the "police riot" during the Democratic National Convention in Chicago, 1968.
- The "Rodney King" trial in California in which the police officers involved were found "not guilty"—insane!—and then the federal trial which followed; the latter violated the U.S. Constitutional prohibition against "double jeopardy" (regardless of anyone's legal hairsplitting)—even more insane!!
- The massacres at Ruby Ridge, Idaho in 1992 and Waco, Texas in 1993 and the circus of handwringing, inquiries, cover-ups and trials which followed.
- The events which led to the sinking of the *Lusitania* (which influenced the entry of the U.S. into World War I).
- The Gulf of Tonkin "incident" and the Vietnam War in general.
- All lawyer "jokes".
- All commercials and advertisements.

Appendix II

A Toxick Chaos Virus Rite
by Rev. Dagon

Over a decade ago, after reading through the first edition of *The Psychopath's Bible*, (initially released as *The Toxick Magician*), I contemplated many courses of action that could be taken using the philosophies and tools of Toxick Magick. A discussion between a fellow Frater, the late William S. Burroughs, brought to light an opportunity that appeared ripe for such an approach.

A certain Reverend, who for liability purposes we shall name Rev. Ned Yelps, had a penchant for conducting campaigns of hatred and harassment against homosexuals and victims of AIDS. In the years prior to our decision to take action to manipulate the Rev. Yelps, he had been successful in attracting a rather large contingent of followers in the Midwest. Their *modus operandi* was to blanket-fax the media and picket the businesses and funerals of homosexuals and persons infected or killed by the AIDS virus with such messages as "Gods Hates Fags", "We Hate Homos", etc. In our research, we also uncovered that the Rev. Yelps was a disbarred lawyer and had been convicted of child abuse—which was a sure sign that the Rev. Yelps had a soft underbelly, ripe for evisceration.

Utilizing the Toxic Magick techniques of feeding the victim's ego and using it against him covertly, as well as a bit of subterfuge in disarming the victim with a false honesty and admiration, we infiltrated the Rev. Yelps organization via email and phone conversations. Our goal was to create a situation wherein the victim and his organization would destroy themselves through their own actions.

As a basis for our action, we utilized the concept of a "Chaos Virus." Chaos Virii are similar to Chaos Servitors[1] in that they are entities capable of functioning independently of the magician—an independent thoughtform or Tulpa. One trait that Chaos Virii exhibit is that they replicate themselves by feeding off the host. This is not necessarily the case with Chaos Servitors unless they are specifically programmed to do so.

A Chaos Virus does not necessarily need to have a specified length of life, unless so desired, since their life span is contingent on the life of their host(s) or their host's defenses. Therefore Chaos Virii have a built-in self-destruct mode since they die when the host dies or they are killed off by the host's defenses. Construction of a Chaos Virus should incorporate characteristics of the AIDS virus, at least to the extent that the AIDS virus is immune to human defense systems.

Included in the following ritual rubric are examples from a Chaos Virus Rite performed for the purpose of infiltrating and subverting a well-known homophobic Christian evangelist, The Rev. Ned Yelps.

This rite was an exercise in utilizing the Internet and phone as tools of Toxick Magick. Research, infiltration and infection were all accomplished utilizing FTP searches, email, and phone conversations/messages. Prior to the rite, contact with the host, through the Rev. Yelps' brother-in-law, was made undercover via email and telephone. The text of the initial letter and reply was as follows:

> Dear Mr. XXXXXXX,
>
> After perusing numerous ftp archives, I came across many files with derogatory statements regarding you, Rev. Yelps and the XXXXX Baptist church. These faggots make me sick and I wanted you to know that I, and many of my friends, support your agenda. We have to stop these homo hoards from taking over the country, the media and the gov't.

---

[1] See Phil Hine's *Condensed Chaos* and *Prime Chaos*; Peter Carroll's *PsyberMagick*; and Lawrence Galian's *Beyond Duality*.

We are starting a magazine called "WE SHALL OVERCOME" and we would be interested in a phone interview with Rev. Yelps. Hopefully, this would be aired on a local radio station and subsequently transcribed to be included in our magazine. If Rev. Yelps is interested, we would be glad to include any questions that Rev. Yelps would like us to ask in the interview. If you could email me a reply at xxx@xxxx.xxx with a confirmation of Rev. Yelps' interest in doing an interview, questions, time and phone number we could contact him at, it would be most appreciated.

Yours Sincerely,

XXXXXXX

Dear Mr. XXXXXXX:

I must admit that I find this to be a bit shocking, for seldom is support found coming into my email box. I am sure that Mr. Yelps, Sr. would be happy to do a radio interview with you. You can reach him at XXX XXX XXXX by leaving a message on his answering machine. His mailing address is P.O. Box XXXX, Topeka, KS XXXXX.

As I am sure you are aware, we are very cautious as to whom we give out information, including interviews. Please do not take this to be anything but caution on our part. I would be interested in receiving information from you regarding where you are, more about your organization, etc. Nothing personal is necessary, just information about your organization, etc.

On a personal note, where are you finding the information about us through ftp? I'm interested in seeing the articles myself, as I'm sure I don't see even a small fraction of what is out there.

Again, let me express my surprise at this invitation. I am sure that if you call Fred Sr. and leave the message on his machine he would be willing to speak to you when it is convenient.

Please do not hesitate to email me at this address with more information.

Proud to be Homophobic

XXXXXXX X. XXXXXX

This set the stage for contact and subsequent infection through the Branch Yelpsians compound and cohorts.

The Chaos Virus Rite

Pre-Ritual (to be performed prior to the rite, either for a day, a week, or a month):

1. Focus on oneself as an eating, drinking, sleeping, speaking, fornicating creature.

2. Radically change, alter, stop any or all of the above for a specified period of time before the ritual.

Ritual Preparation

1. Construct a mantric and symbolic sigil of the intent, purpose and action of the Chaos Virus.

2. A sturdy staff or rod.

3. Relevant incense, music, strobe lights, fog, etc.

4. Acquire a Television you are willing to sacrifice for use in this rite.

    a. Prepare T.V. by painting a chaos star with a Chaos Virus Sigil in the center of the screen.

Ritual

Statement of Intent: ("It is our will to create a Chaos Virus to...")

For this rite the statement of intent was:

It is our will to create a Chaos Virus that will cause the Reverend Ned Yelps and his followers to make fools of themselves in the media and ruin their credibility and success in their goals.

This intent was condensed into the mantra: "BO-IS-E-NAW" and the sigil: "*", an asterisk which was inspired by Kurt Vonnegut's book *Breakfast with Champions* where the asterisk is likened to a human asshole. The asterisk, being a sublime symbol, was easily embedded in a letter or email.

1. Light incense; turn on the TV to static with the sound turned all the way up; strobe lights on; fog machine spewing; and any other effects to create a theatrical circus atmosphere.

2. All participants sit in a half circle in front of the prepared TV with the staff (rod) in the center.

a. For this rite, the Virus Sigil to be charged was an asterisk (painted within a chaos star on the screen of the TV set.)

3. All start mimicking the behavior of the host.

In this rite, we exhibited homophobic behavior by stomping around and screaming in a fanatical fashion statements such as: "God hates fags!", "Sodomites belong in hell!", "We Hate Homos!" This aligns the group with the host and programs the virus to appear benign, non-harmful and sympathetic, thereby allowing access to the host.

4. Each participant then invokes a different godform related to the rite, not a full invocation but more overshadowing (see *Prime Chaos* by Phil Hine) or intense visualizations and theatrics.

For this rite, we utilized god forms of the Greek and Roman pantheon (Dionysus, Apollo, Hermes, Ganymede and Zeus), because of the prevalence and acceptance of homo-/bi-sexuality and power within those archetypes.

5. All participants then move back into a half-circle in front of the TV, kneeling, and all grabbing the staff/rod. All then start stroking the staff as if masturbating a phallus and chanting phrases incongruent to the host, something you want the host to do/act/say. Each participant chants only one phrase repeatedly.

a. For this rite, we utilized phrases such as "Jesus was an ass fucker", "God loves fags", "Jehovah eats man cum", "Jesus licks my dick", etc.

6. Continue to glossalalia.

7. At the height of glossalalia and staff stroking, all pick up the staff and stare into the Chaos Star Virus sigil and yell the mantric sigil of the Chaos Virus purpose, "BO-IS-E-NAW," while smashing the staff into the center of the Chaos Star Virus Sigil on the TV screen, charging/programming the Virus.

8. Banish with laughter

9. Send the sigil in a letter through the mail, email or in a phone message for infection.

A letter was sent via email with the Chaos Virus imbedded therein, as well as in a call made to Rev. Yelps' answering machine. The phone message thanked the Rev. Yelps for the opportunity for an interview but, at this time, the magazine and interview had been indefinitely put on hold to take care of other business. The Toxick mantric sigil was sublimely chanted in the background of the message.

This particular version of the rite was rather successful in that, the day following the rite, Rev. Yelps and his contingent of picketers with signs such as "God hates Fags", "Homos belong in Hell", etc. were run out of Lawrence, Kansas. This was the first occurrence of a negative backlash at one of Rev. Yelps' anti-gay rallies. A month later, Rev. Yelps was a guest on the Ricki Lake Show and was thoroughly ridiculed and laughed at for his beliefs and actions. A few years later, a news segment on the Rev. Yelps and his group was aired on TV relating how Rev. Yelps' group was going to picket a coffee shop that employed homosexuals. The coffee shop owners turned the tables on Rev. Yelps' group by sponsoring a benefit wherein every hour the Rev. Yelps' group picketed the coffee shop; the coffee shop patrons would make a donation to an AIDS charity. The Rev. Yelps did not show up and only five members of his group stood outside for only a few hours—earning the AIDS charity a few thousand dollars. This approach has since been used against Rev. Yelps' protesters on a number of occasions.

The Rev. Yelps' group recently initiated a flyer campaign and protest against the constant "Hate Crimes," violence and vandalism against Rev. Yelps' church membership with little sympathy from the local authorities. The hilarity continues with protests against the benevolent children's television personality Mr. Rogers. Rev. Yelps' daughter was quoted in the press stating, "This country has forgotten God and effectively flipped him off and Mr. Rogers is in part responsible."

It appears that a chemical cocktail to cure the spread of the Toxick Virus has not been discovered by Rev. Yelps and his group... Maybe a Kool-aid virus à la Jim Jones is in order.

Appendix III

Nightmares & Other Trivia:
The Psychopath's Contest

Develop one or more of the following "seed ideas." Send your work to us along with a release to use it and whether or not you would like us to include your name. We will include the best in the next edition.

CPCXYXY.2: Sex—what price?

The great secret to control is: diminish pleasure, increase guilt. Happy people cannot be controlled. Guilty people demand to be punished. All religions and governments are built on these principles.

Sex has been channeled by all cultures. By controlling sex in various ways people are enslaved.

The price of sex is often destruction of the marginal type. Marriage, children, job, family, etc. are a linear path to the grave. Many marginal types are lost forever in this prison of socialized flesh.

Never pay too much for sex. You are much better off masturbating than getting trapped in marriage (i.e., sex sanctioned by the priest and politician).

You are better off in direct payment than in paying with your life. The entire game is rigged, particularly against potentially powerful males. Simply read the law books.

CPC82478a: For Men

Learn to use sex to achieve power: masturbate often so the psycho-chemical reaction doesn't control you... Practice tantra...any style will do. If you decide on a partner, find one whose nature will enhance you. Keep in mind, however, that once a woman becomes pregnant and has a child, her brain changes. Be alert to the black widow in every mother. More and more male children are being destroyed by "momism"; so if you have a male child be sure that he is trained in sports and that you take a direct hand in raising him. Teach him how to play rough—consider military school, or an all male school out of the country.

Regardless of what any male says, women are first mother-images. So the label "wife" is a substitute mother-figure who he is allowed to have sex with. Getting married to a highly socialized female will cost you more than 50% of your life. The children are hers, you are hers. Your value is the contribution of sperm, money and status. Always keep in mind that most females are agents for the social fabric and, in this sense, "work" for the culture.

CPC82478b: For Women

Some potentially powerful women have been ruined by marriage with children... I personally know of two cases, and there is very little we can do to reverse the social-chemical process.

If you pick men for their power, what does that leave for you? If you pick men for their competence and self-esteem, you invite your own development.

"In order to say 'I love you,' you must first be say to say 'I'." (Ayn Rand)

Multiple Motives

People do things for multiple reasons. However, we tend to look for "The Motive." And we usually accept the most sinister. The rule here is to help people find your "real" motive while keeping hidden your other motives. First you have to know most of your own motives. Then, by selective misdirection, help other people discover the one you want them to believe. People will assume the motive you deny is the real motive. If someone of authority tells them what your real motive is, they will tend to believe it. If your motive seems "selfish" they will believe it. And so on.

Pre-emptive Strikes

If someone is about to accuse you—or is accusing you—of something sinister, pre-empt them by admitting to a lesser offense. Switch the motive they are attributing to you, change the timing, but give them something to criticize. No one will believe that you are *completely* innocent, so always plead guilty to a lesser "crime." Accept responsibility for *something*, even if it is something as simple as ignorance. Apologize for things you didn't do. It makes people happy to find your faults.

Misdirection

This is an innate survival technique of most animals. Most people are fair at this game; however, adding conscious misdirection is good training. It will help your thinking process and possibly teach you how to cover up your fears and anxiety.

In poker, misdirection is a primary strategy. Checking at the right time with a losing or winning hand; checking and raising, again at the right time; bluffing: all of these simple techniques are based on the power of misdirection. You allow other people to jump to their own conclusions......everybody loves to be a prophet and predict the future. Allow them to do this a few times and, when it is worth your while, simply fool them by not doing what they expect.

Prediction and the Illusion of Control

The popularity of astrology assures us that it is more important to have the *illusion* that you can predict and are in charge than it is to *actually* predict accurately and be in charge. Never argue with people who use more or less useless techniques......let them do it. In fact, help them. Buy them books on subjects which give them the illusion that they can predict the future and are in control. For example, with a person who believes in astrology, provide them with information they made have missed. Assure them of their abilities and then use it against them: if a person says that Mercury is retrograde, then take advantage of them at that time and let them attribute it to Mercury's being retrograde.

Let Them Give You Reasons

Avoid arguing with the reasons people give you—they are usually just complaining and creating illusions. Just shake your head and say, "Yes I understand" and then do what you want anyway. I often use this technique in real estate or other large purchases. I agree with them in subtle ways, giving them the impression that their item is worth more than it is, and then offer what I want.

Delusions Everywhere

As humans are "causal hungry," they attribute causality to either internal causes (me) or otherwise (not me). It doesn't matter whether the attribution is true or false. I am discussing attribution styles:

— "All events are caused by me"; very rare and delusional.

— "All events are caused by other forces"; very rare and delusional.

— "Good events are caused by me, bad events are caused by not me"; very immature. (The good me, bad you.)

— "Bad events are caused by me, good events are caused by not me"; very immature. (The bad me, good you.)

— The objective type—scientific type, very rare indeed—no moral implication.

Most commonly, some events are caused by me and others are not. Remember that any explanation doesn't—and I repeat, *doesn't*—have to be accurate for anyone......

Keep in mind the importance of style and manipulating style... Also keep in mind that people assume that the ability to explain something means that they have influence over the "something."

If you get a person to believe the attribution you have created, you have also gotten them to believe that either they or you can influence that "something."

Example 1:

John is in a bad mood; his girlfriend refused to go to a party with him... John is an externalizer; that is, he attributes the "why" she won't go to external forces. You pick up a newspaper and tell him that Mercury is retrograde and that this is the likely cause why his girlfriend refused him.

John has heard of astrology; you continue with your explanation of "why his girlfriend won't go with him." He shows signs that he believes this. Your next step is to get him to pay for a chart of his girlfriend's sign so he will know when she is more likely to go along with what he wants. His mood lifts as he is writing you a check. It doesn't matter that the reason she won't go is that she is trying to break off the relationship. Even when John finds out later that this is what she is doing, you inform him that by having her chart and buying another on himself, he will increase his chances of halting the termination of the relationship.

When the relationship ends and John approaches you with this fact, you say you are sorry, but when you analyze the position of Venus and Mars in their charts you inform him that their relationship was doomed from the very beginning and that he is better off. John is disappointed but he knows two things. First, he knows the cause; and second, he knows it wasn't his fault.

Example 2:

Bill has been diagnosed with diabetes. He is an internalizer; that is, he believes that he is the cause of most things. You inform him that it is his bad living habits that have caused the diabetes. You might even say that he had a genetic predisposition, but that his lifestyle is at fault. You suggest that he change his diet and exercise and present him with a contract to a health spa. Bill signs the contract because you have provided him with a cause that he can accept. First, it is his fault and, because it is his fault and he now knows the cause, he can do something about it. Although exercise and diet will, in fact, help, it will not "cure" the disease. But what it did cure was Bill's need to know that the cause is under his control.

What are some of the factors which make both Jim and Bill accept your attributions?

First you are credible: you look as if you have power.

Second, your explanation sounds reasonable within the social/cultural matrix of the subject.

Third, you have given them both a sense that they have some way of controlling the future: John, by understanding charts and Bill by doing exercise and diet.

End Note

Does this man look like a child abuser?

Yes, no or maybe? Circle your answer now!

MORE FROM CHRISTOPHER S. HYATT, Ph.D.

SECRETS OF WESTERN TANTRA
The Sexuality of the Middle Path

Introduced by J.M. Spiegelman, Ph.D.
Preface by Robert Anton Wilson

Dr. Hyatt reveals secret methods of enlightenment through transmutation of the *orgastic reflex*. Filled with explicit, practical techniques.

"The world's first scientific experimental yoga that does not expurgate the sensory-sensual-sexual aspects of the Great Work."
—Robert Anton Wilson

ISBN 1-56184-113-7

SEX MAGICK, TANTRA & TAROT
The Way of the Secret Lover

With Lon Milo DuQuette
Illustrated by David P. Wilson

A wealth of practical and passionate Tantric techniques utilizing the Archetypal images of the Tarot. Nothing is held back. All methods are explicit and clearly described.

"Each of us has a Guardian Angel — a companion and lover who waits just behind the images that flood our minds during sleep or reverie."

ISBN 1-56184-044-0

MORE FROM CHRISTOPHER S. HYATT, PH.D.

UNDOING YOURSELF WITH ENERGIZED MEDITATION

Introduced by Dr. Israel Regardie
Preface by Robert Anton Wilson

A new edition of Dr. Hyatt's incredible, ground-breaking book with 64 pages of brand new material.

"...the Energized Meditation system is fun and erotic and makes you smarter..." Extensively illustrated.

"*Undoing Yourself* is the latest attempt by the Illuminati Conspiracy to reveal the hither-to hidden teachings." — Robert Anton Wilson

ISBN 1-56184-057-2

PACTS WITH THE DEVIL
A Chronicle of Sex, Blasphemy & Liberation

With S. Jason Black

Braving the new Witchcraft Panic that is sweeping America, *Pacts With The Devil* places the Western magical tradition and the Western psyche in perspective. Contains a detailed history of European 'Black Magic' and includes new editions of 17th and 18th century Grimoires with detailed instruction for their use. Extensively illustrated.

ISBN 1-56184-058-0

MORE FROM CHRISTOPHER S. HYATT, Ph.D.

URBAN VOODOO
*A Beginner's Guide to
Afro-Caribbean Magic*
With S. Jason Black

Voodoo, Santeria and Macumba as practiced today in cities throughout the Western world. Includes descriptions of the phenomena triggered by Voodoo practice, divination techniques, spells and a method of self-initiation. Illustrated.

ISBN 1-56184-059-9

ALEISTER CROWLEY'S ILLUSTRATED GOETIA
Sexual Evocation
With Aleister Crowley &
Lon Milo DuQuette
Illustrated by David P. Wilson

'Goetia [refers to] all the operations of that Magick which deals with gross, malignant or unenlightened forces.' Crowley's *Goetia* is brought to life with vivid illustrations of the demons. Commentary by Crowley experts DuQuette and Hyatt bring the ancient arts into the modern day.

ISBN 1-56184-048-3

MORE FROM CHRISTOPHER S. HYATT, PH.D.

TABOO
Sex, Religion & Magic

With Lon DuQuette & Gary Ford

Introduced by Robert Anton Wilson

The extensive case histories and rituals expose the *unspeakable taboo* of the West: the union of sex and religion.

"I think it is safe to say that every organized group of idiots will regard this book as extremely dangerous."
                —Robert Anton Wilson

ISBN 1-56184-039-4

THE TREE OF LIES
Become Who You Are

Introduced by Robert Anton Wilson

The Tree of Lies takes us on a walking tour of the prison erected by the lies that society tells us and the lies we tell ourselves. And then it provides the tools to tunnel out.

"Is it possible to use language to undo the hallucinations created by language? ...a few heroic efforts seem able to jolt readers awake... to transcend words."
                —Robert Anton Wilson

ISBN 1-56184-008-4

TECHNIQUES FOR UNDOING YOURSELF VOL. I (2 CDs)

With S. Jason Black, Zehm Aloim and Israel Regardie

The first in a series of CDs in which Dr. Hyatt presents effective methods to change your self and your life! A great companion to Hyatt's ground-breaking book, *Undoing Yourself With Energized Meditation and Other Devices;* adds an entirely new dimension to your repertoire of powerful and dynamic methods of self-change.

ISBN 1-56184-280-X

THE MAGIC OF ISRAEL REGARDIE (2 CDs)

With Zehm Aloim

A frank, in-depth discussion of the many facets and beliefs of one of the world's great mystical adepts, Israel Regardie. Regardie, the author of *The Complete Golden Dawn System of Magic* and many other works, is rightfully considered the greatest proponent of the Golden Dawn. Christopher Hyatt lived and worked with Regardie and knew him better than anyone alive today.

ISBN 1-56184-230-3